D0112680

CHOOSE
STOCKS WISELY

A FORMULA THAT PRODUCED AMAZING RETURNS

BY DR. PAUL W. ALLEN

FOREWORD BY ETHAN POPE

An important message from the author: This book is not intended to give *specific* investment counsel. Its purpose is to give general insight into the area of investing in common stocks while clarifying the critical role of the balance sheet in assessing risk. All principles and/ or methods covered are not to be taken as specific recommendations for any individual or business. The presentation of my personal stock-investing performance in both chart and written format is not intended to represent what a reader can expect from his or her investment decisions. Neither the author nor the publisher can take responsibility for the readers' gains or losses. Should you decide to use the author's system, **he recommends that initially you invest less than 5 percent of your portfolio.** As with all investments, there is the potential to lose money. The specific company stocks that are mentioned in this book are strictly for communicating the author's personal past investing experiences and explaining his balance-sheet buying practice. No specific stock investment is being recommended by the author.

Copyright © 2013 Dr. Paul W. Allen
All rights reserved.

ISBN: 1489542825
ISBN 13: 9781489542823

Library of Congress Control Number: 2013909947
CreateSpace Independent Publishing Platform
North Charleston, South Carolina

TABLE OF CONTENTS

FOREWORD

Few people gain mastery at anything. Paul Allen is an exception to that rule, and one look at his stock portfolio returns confirms it. On February 1, 2003, Paul began investing in the stock market using his system and, according to his Fidelity monthly statements, in just ten years turned approximately $50,000 into $1,320,301. *Of course, Paul's past success is no guarantee of your or my future success in the stock market.*

Everyone dreams about buying stocks at basement prices. In reality, most investors buy high and sell low. Why? Because most investors base their decisions on the latest hot stock tip or emotions such as greed or fear. It appears that Paul has developed a system that is based on facts—facts about the strength of the balance sheet. Paul will teach you how to follow what he calls the balance-sheet formula to selecting stocks.

Here is what I like about Paul's stock-picking system:

1. His system is simple and gives you step-by-step instructions to follow.
2. His system focuses on evaluating a company's balance sheet.
3. His goal is to lower your risk when investing in a stock. Of course, it is impossible for any system to eliminate all the risk.
4. His system will give you a recommended entry-level price for a stock.
5. His system filters out all the media noise and helps you select stocks without following the herd or making emotional picks.

Sounds really simplistic, doesn't it? In some ways, Paul's system is like ordering vanilla ice cream at an ice cream store. It's not flashy, but you know what you are going to get. With ice cream there is room to be adventurous, but, when it comes to money, I'd rather use a vanilla stock-picking system that increases my potential to make money. Taking a wild ride with a mysterious pick-of-the-week flavor can bring significantly more risk of losing money in the stock market. I would choose vanilla ice cream every time.

If you are looking to own stocks that have flashing neon lights or stocks that practically everyone else owns, Paul's system is not for you. He looks for solid companies that are seldom in the news or on most investors' radar screens.

I asked Paul, "Why are you sharing your system with everyone?" His response sums up the man that he is. "My desire is to help people avoid the mistakes and financial losses I experienced earlier in life. It hurts to lose money in the stock market, not only financially, but spiritually. You experience pain and guilt. Using my method, I believe I can help people select stocks that have great potential for gain and less potential for loss. Why would I want to hoard my system and keep it a secret? The life of a steward should be one of sharing and generosity."

Now that Paul's book is in print, I am eager to give his stock-picking system a test drive. My plan is to begin by investing a small portion of my portfolio using his system. If it works, I will continue to use it. If you plan to give Paul's system a test drive, you should do the same and see how the system works for you. I like the fact that Paul recommends you begin by investing less than 5 percent of your portfolio.

Don't view Paul's system as a get-rich-quick strategy or a guarantee that you will never lose money. No one, including Paul, can make that guarantee. Paul even explains in his book that he has lost money on stocks—using his system. So remember, Paul's track record is no guarantee that you will have the same results. Any time you invest in the stock market, there is potential for profit *or* loss.

If you are not satisfied with your current stock-picking system or don't have a system, carefully examine Paul's balance-sheet approach and see if it is right for you. By the way, boring vanilla is my favorite ice cream. Over the next few years, I will decide if Paul's vanilla balance-sheet approach to picking stocks becomes my favorite stock-picking system.

Why not dip out a big bowl of vanilla ice cream, dive into this book, and let Paul, who has the heart of a teacher, explain his balance-sheet approach to buying stocks. *Enjoy the ice cream and the book.*

Ethan Pope
Author and Speaker

ACKNOWLEDGMENTS

Many lengthy writing episodes went into the completion of this book. Ethan Pope, financial author, speaker, and radio commentator, provided me with tremendously helpful feedback in the process of taking my initial manuscript draft to a completed work. I did not know Ethan before writing this book. Upon discovering him, I discussed my manuscript with him, and he graciously agreed to review my draft. Since then we have become dear friends, and I can't sufficiently express my appreciation to him for his excellent counsel across the project as the initial draft was honed, and honed again into what I hope is a book that can make a significant contribution to the theme of investing in common stocks.

I would also like to thank Harold Harris, Kathy Little, Dr. Britt McCarty, George Tye, Irvin Florence, and my dear wife, Mickie, for reading the end-stage manuscript and offering their helpful comments, which enabled me to fine-tune the written content in an effort to improve readability. Thanks to my daughter Hannah for working with me on spreadsheet and related issues. Thanks to Jan Herrington and Steve Marks for working with me on some design-based items. I also appreciate my daughter Rebekah for being a good sounding board during my writing.

I'm grateful for the support and encouragement of all my family and friends. Hearing my accounting students, for example, ask me from time to time when my book was going to be finished served to keep me focused.

Thanks to Paul Tarver for his excellent work in the design of my website, www.choosestockswisely.com. Finally, thanks to

CreateSpace personnel who carefully worked with me on publishing the book.

I want this book to be successful because of its message on wise investing. Any success will be, in no small measure, due to those people God put in my life to encourage and help me along the way.

Dr. Paul W. Allen

An important message from the author: This book is not intended to give *specific* investment counsel. Its purpose is to give general insight into the area of investing in common stocks while clarifying the critical role of the balance sheet in assessing risk. All principles and/or methods covered are not to be taken as specific recommendations for any individual or business. The presentation of my personal stock-investing performance in both chart and written format is not intended to represent what a reader can expect from his or her investment decisions. Neither the author nor the publisher can take responsibility for the readers' gains or losses. Should you decide to use the author's system, **he recommends that initially you invest less than 5 percent of your portfolio.** As with all investments, there is the potential to lose money. The specific company stocks that are mentioned in this book are strictly for communicating the author's personal past investing experiences and explaining his balance-sheet buying practice. No specific stock investment is being recommended by the author.

CHAPTER 1

INTRODUCTION

Anyone considering "investing" time and money into this book would naturally wonder what the writer has to say about buying stocks that has not already been said. Why should you want to read this book? Permit me to uncomfortably engage in a bit of bragging to capture your attention. My personal portfolio has outpaced every major index by many percentage points in performance and has done so over virtually any time horizon one might utilize during the past decade. My early retirement at age fifty-four on June 30, 2010, is a direct result of stock investment returns achieved. Now I can pursue other things—such as, for one, writing this book.

My first attempts at selecting my own investments in the stock market were a miserable failure, but after careful consideration I developed the balance-sheet buying strategy, a "lower the risk" stock-selection strategy that has exponentially increased my returns. Just how great has my success been using this buying strategy? Looking at a long-term ten-year window that started on February 1, 2003, when I first adopted my buying strategy and ended on January 31, 2013, my five-year and ten-year annualized returns are 14.48 percent and 38.73 percent, respectively. This compares with five-year and ten-year returns on the S&P 500 across the identical February 1, 2003, to January 31, 2013, time horizon of 3.97 percent and 7.93 percent, respectively.

Fidelity Investments is the online brokerage firm I used for investing in stocks across the entire ten-year time horizon, and all percentage return data on my personal account versus the S&P 500 is supplied by Fidelity. Fidelity is the only firm I have used for my stock investing. Fidelity has not advised me on any of the stock purchases made. The returns achieved above were gained by my sole investment choices based on the balance-sheet buying approach I developed. The approach permitted me to multiply my invested capital more than twenty-six times from February 1, 2003, to January 31, 2013. I turned approximately $50,000 into $1,320,301 during those ten years.

The chart below shows my investment performance, achieved by closely adhering to my buying strategy.

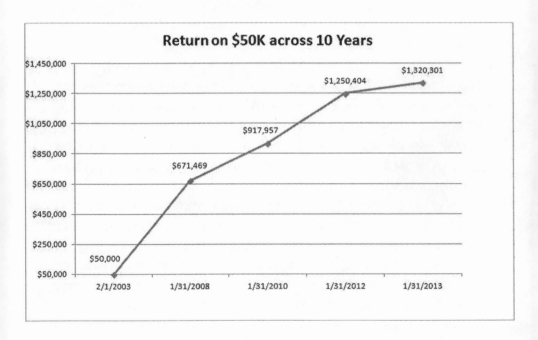

My above-average returns, which included the very diffi-cult recessionary market of 2008 into early 2009, can only be explained by the benefits of buying deep-value stocks based on proper assessment of the balance sheet, a practice that is espe-cially important in difficult economic times and accompanying market downturns when faltering earnings are commonplace among businesses.

In this book you will read the formula to my success: my goal in writing is to share it with you. Certainly, to make money in the stock market, you have to sell stocks to realize any gains. However the key to my high returns is the balance-sheet, lower-the-risk buying strategy I follow strictly. It tells me when a stock price is low, enabling me to avoid "unnecessary" risk when buy-ing. This book does not cover the topic of selling stocks—it is strictly focused on my balance-sheet buying strategy (formula), which is, again, the reason behind my extraordinary stock returns. My balance-sheet buying strategy is focused on buying quality stocks at low prices.

> This book does not cover the topic of selling stocks—it is strictly focused on my balance-sheet buying strategy (formula), which is, again, the reason behind my extraordinary stock returns.

Throughout the book, I believe my background as a col-lege accounting professor will be apparent. Also obvious will be my Christian faith. Some people may believe that investing in common stocks is contrary to the will of God and that He is not interested in money or how we manage it. In my view, God is very much interested in how we manage the financial resources He entrusts to our care. Sound money management is essential knowledge for responsible stewardship and the sort of financial independence needed to avoid being taken advantage of by those less-scrupulous members of society. This is not to say, however, that every person should have an interest in investing in common stocks. Investing in common stocks is one investing alternative among many.

In Matthew, chapter 25, verses 14–30, of the Bible, we read what is known as the parable of the talents. In this passage, Jesus tells a story of three servants who are given stewardship responsibility over their master's talents while the master leaves on a journey. During the master's time away, two of the servants invest the master's resources and double the resources entrusted to their keeping. The other servant buries in the ground the resources entrusted to him. When the master returns from his journey, he is pleased with the two wise servants who, by putting the resources to work, doubled the amounts entrusted to them. However, the master is displeased with the servant who foolishly buried the resources entrusted to his care and made no effort to generate a return for the master. The first two servants yielded a significant return on the master's resources while the third servant provided no return.

The parable of the talents gives us God's perspective toward good stewardship. First, from the parable, we can see that the resources or blessings we have, including our money, come from God. Second, God wants us to put those resources to work. As Christians, if we are to be found faithful, we must employ the various talents, including monetary resources that God entrusts to our care so that His kingdom can prosper. In the New King James Version of the Bible, I Corinthians 4:5, the apostle Paul writes:

"Moreover it is required in stewards that one be found faithful."

The Lord has granted me much success in my stock-market investments. During my life, I have migrated from thinking about investing in the stock market as gambling to understanding that it can be a source of significant investment returns if one invests wisely. The parable of the talents does not teach us that risk-taking is wrong. In fact, it teaches us that our resources come from God and that we should put them to work for Him. The passage from Matthew tells us that the steward who was lazy and buried the talent entrusted to him was "afraid." We should never be afraid to obey God. However, we must invest wisely if we are to achieve a return.

Again, there are many alternative monetary investment options available to people today, and investing in common stocks is not for everyone. For those who are interested in learning more about investing in common stocks, it is my intention to describe my formula for buying "wisely." My success with stocks reflects an understanding of how to take justifiable risks in seeking solid investment returns. I believe my approach to buying stocks is consistent with practicing responsible stewardship. I had to learn some tough lessons first, which are detailed in chapter 2.

Allow me to preview a couple of my stock success stories now, which I address in more detail in chapter 8. Small companies have generally achieved the greatest returns for me. I bought Forward Industries (FORD) during 2003 and 2004 at an average cost of about $2 a share and sold for over $25 a share in 2005. I acquired DXP Enterprises (DXPE) from 2003 to 2005 at an average cost of about $4 a share and netted well over a 1,000 percent gain by my final sale in 2008. These success stories are a direct result of my balance-sheet, lower-the-risk formula to buying stocks.

If you have an interest in the stock market and want to learn how to buy stocks low, this book is for you. The only way to consistently make money in the stock market is to consistently buy low. Buying low is more important than selling high. If you buy low, your odds of making money are strong even if you don't sell at the highs.

> **If you have an interest in the stock market and want to learn how to buy stocks low, this book is for you.**

Buying low—or getting a bargain through a stock price relative to the value it offers—is not determined simply by the size of the share price number. A $100 stock price on a given company may be lower relative to the actual value of the stock than is a $2 ticket price on a share of common stock of a different company. This book will show the balance sheet to be the great equalizer for leveling the playing field on companies when assessing whether a stock is trading at a low price given its inherent value.

To become better at buying stocks when they are undervalued, you must learn how to interpret a balance sheet. Risk is the potential downside. Buying low means that risk has already been largely factored into the stock price when you buy, thereby greatly improving the potential for significant upside. Proper risk assessment helps an investor have a better idea of where the "floor" is, and therefore helps minimize any loss if things don't pan out on the reward side. In this book, I will show how the balance sheet can be used to identify a truly cheap stock price, not a cheap (worthless) stock.

The chapters ahead explain the balance sheet's critical role in assessing risk in a practical way. After you read this book and see what I do to identify a quality stock selling at a low price, I believe you will feel much better informed about how to use a corporation's balance sheet to identify a low buying price on a common stock of interest. Buying good stocks at low prices greatly improves the chances of making some solid investment returns while lessening the prospect of losing hard-earned dollars and cents.

Please note that any specific stock that appears anywhere in this book does not reflect a recommendation to buy or sell that stock. Specific stocks are mentioned only for developing my message, which is how to identify quality stocks trading at low prices by using the balance sheet as your primary tool in risk assessment.

CHAPTER 2

LEARN IT OR LOSE IT

Do not store up for yourselves treasures on earth, where moths and vermin destroy, and where thieves break in and steal. But store up for yourselves treasures in heaven, where moths and vermin do not destroy, and where thieves do not break in and steal.
—Matthew 6:19–20 (New International Version)

The scripture quotations at the beginning of some chapters in this book reflect biblical truths. These truths apply to all aspects of life, including investing in common stocks. For instance, according to the above scripture from Matthew, if I invest money into stocks carelessly, without any sense of responsibility toward others, void of a sense of stewardship in deciding how and where it is invested, it is likely to be lost. Conversely, if it is invested with a sense of stewardship and purpose beyond that of just building up my worldly possessions, my decision making will be more responsible, and the likelihood of losing money from foolish investments greatly diminished.

This first chapter covers some personal background that has brought me to where I am today with investing in common stocks—personal history that is probably similar to the stories of many others who have invested in the stock market for an extensive period and know what it feels like to have experienced significant losses at some point.

This chapter will read like an autobiography of sorts. In addition to providing background into how my years of accounting education were converted into a real-world, how-to approach to buying common stocks, it serves to introduce me to you, the reader, in a manner that, hopefully, will allow you to identify with me throughout the book. The years I've been privileged to be teaching in the college classroom have made me keenly aware of how important being "real" with the students is for learning to take place.

This chapter tells how I got into purchasing common stocks and about the early mistakes I made due to a lack of practical understanding of proper risk assessment—mistakes that resulted in substantial loss of invested capital. It then describes the events leading to the development of my current balance-sheet buying formula, which has resulted in performance that consistently exceeds market results.

One major benefit of learning a difficult lesson is finding out something useful to pass along to the next person to enable him or her to avoid the same mistakes. Learning from mistakes is a great thing, but it is even better to learn how to avoid making mistakes.

My personal history shows that without a substantive approach to buying common stocks, a person can lose hard-earned money, but that with a solid risk-assessment approach, significant returns are probable. After I describe the events that led to my developing such an approach, I will, beginning with chapter 3, discuss the balance sheet as the essential analysis tool to be utilized when buying common stocks and develop that discussion throughout the remainder of the book.

Is Stock Investing Like Gambling?

I was raised by parents who grew up during the Great Depression. They were hard-working people who had to scrounge for every penny for a substantial part of their lives. When they realized any savings, they resorted to buying certificates of deposit (CDs) at banks to achieve a return on those savings. During my youthful years, all I knew about investing was the world of CDs. The most important lessons I learned from my parents about money while growing up were that you should work hard and do a good job to earn money, you should practice saving money, and giving money to the Lord's work brings honor to God.

Later on, while pursuing my doctoral degree in accounting when I was in my thirties, some of my finance courses challenged certain acquired beliefs—such as the beliefs that investing in anything riskier than a CD was foolish and that investing in the stock market was gambling. As I learned more about the relationship of risk and return, it became apparent that there is a real difference between gambling and investing in common stocks.

With investing in common stocks, you have access to all sorts of information that can be used in risk assessment versus potential return. For example, you have access to financial statements of publicly-traded companies, information you can use to assess how much risk you would be taking relative to return that might be achieved. When investors properly use available information, the expected outcome from investing in common stocks should be positive. Otherwise, the investment should not be made. With gambling, your expected outcome is negative. The gambler, then, is a risk seeker, while the common-stock investor seeks to avoid risk that is unlikely to be rewarded fairly. The stock investor's risk aversion leads to taking care to avoid putting money in a stock unless it's likely to eventually realize more than was put in it.

Also, with gambling, you have a winner and a loser, and money gets transferred from one party to the other. With investing in a corporation's common stock, it is plausible that most investors may benefit along with their company if the firm performs well and the stock price trends higher over the long stretch of time. That is, it can be a winning situation all the way around, rather than a zero-sum game as with gambling, where one party wins at the expense of the other.

It also eventually occurred to me that if everyone viewed investing in common stocks as gambling, there would be inadequate capital for businesses to form and operate as corporations, resulting in a mass of people not having jobs, which would feed through our economic system with devastating effects. So my mind was changed. I was ready and willing to diversify away from CDs with my own personal savings into some common stocks. Over the next several years, I was about to learn a difficult lesson, though, on the difference between knowing *about* the need for risk assessment before buying stocks and knowing *how* to perform proper risk assessment before buying stocks.

Initial Foray into Stock Investing

It was about 1992 or so when my change of heart led me into the stock market. Looking at pretty charts in my doctoral finance classes—charts that showed the Dow Jones Index, for example, sloping ever upward over decades of time—gave me the false impression that if one bought some stocks and just held, eventually those stocks would outperform CDs for sure. It also seemed reasonable that one could select individual stocks over mutual funds and achieve better relative returns since mutual funds can be over-diversified. Finance classes taught me that it takes around twenty stocks to maximize the benefits of diversification; since many mutual funds own hundreds of stocks, they are probably over-diversified.

I was overlooking one big problem with my buying of individual stocks: I was no expert stock-picker yet, and that is an understatement! I had some general ideas about risk and return but definitely had not yet learned the art of proper risk assessment through balance-sheet analysis.

So I put some money into a few stocks. Fortunately, at this time of my life, I did not have a whole lot of money to invest. The few stocks I started with plummeted within a couple of years' time. My doctoral classes had showed me that the future expected earnings of a company drive the direction of the company's future stock price. The earnings projections on the stocks I had bought were good and justified my purchasing them—based on my textbook knowledge attained in college finance courses. However, the actual earnings did not pan out as expected, and the stocks declined significantly below the prices I paid.

What could I have done to avoid the outcome of substantial loss of my invested capital? At the time I purchased the stocks, how could I have compensated for the potential failure of expected earnings to materialize? After all, no one has that kind of crystal ball. Clearly, something was missing from my practical understanding of how to assess my risk when buying common stocks.

I had worked hard for the money I lost. The loss was unpleasant, but the sense of irresponsibility and stewardship failure was overwhelming. The money was gone, and there was absolutely nothing to show for it. There were people I could have helped with the money that was lost. Had I taken a calculated risk? My investment losses shouted that I had not.

Today I know that looking forward at earnings can help in speculating on where a stock price could head next and is useful in assessing potential stock return or reward, but it does not do much for assessing the risk, or potential downside, present in a stock price at any particular point. Clearly, the stocks I purchased had substantial risk that escaped my analysis. That is, my investment losses suggested I had not purchased "low." I needed to figure out the true meaning of "buying low."

The scripture quoted at the start of this chapter came to mind. The next thought went something like this: had I been more stewardship-minded, I would have been more careful with my investment activity with regard to risk analysis. That is, I needed to better understand the potential downside to any investment before taking a financial stake. I realized that my analysis approach needed major improvement before I put hard-earned money into common stocks again. I needed to understand my investing choices much better and have a substantive basis for believing that I was buying low.

If buying stocks occurs on an impulsive whim, like what can happen when one just follows the herd, for example, clearly no real basis in the form of a calculated risk exists that permits the buying to be called investing. It is not that investing in stocks is gambling; rather, without proper risk assessment, buying common stocks is not investing and might as well be viewed as gambling.

It is not that investing in stocks is gambling; rather, without proper risk assessment, buying common stocks is not investing and might as well be viewed as gambling.

My stock-investing experiences up to this time seemed like gambling to me because I had not yet learned the key to proper risk assessment. Buying a stock does not automatically make one an investor, if the word *investor* has any real meaning. I can dress up like a professional golfer and buy all the golf equipment used by the best pros, but all it would take for people to know I'm not a great golfer is a single swing of the club. A person who plays golf well has put in the time to learn how to swing the golf club, which club to select for the next shot, how to factor in elements such as wind, and has practiced, practiced, practiced. Similarly, to become a good investor requires learning how to invest and then honing those investing skills through practice.

After my initial losses, for the remaining years of the twentieth century and into the start of the twenty-first, saving money was a focal point of financial planning. As a result of my difficult stock-investing experiences, I invested in highly certain CDs.

Perhaps the most important lesson I learned from the stock losses was a spiritual one that led to immediate change in my life. The verses from Matthew quoted above led to me having a greater heart for giving to help meet the needs of others. After losing money from those stock investments, I realized how differently I would have felt if I had simply given the money I lost to honor God and be used by Him to meet the needs of other people. I would have not had that great sense of loss, but rather the satisfaction of helping people who needed financial support. Giving all your money away is not my point here. Giving should be done responsibly. My point is that failing to understand the risk in an investment is equivalent to throwing your money away. My giving habits changed as a result of the investing lesson learned—and my investing habits were soon to change.

Second Venture into the Stock Market

We all lived through Y2K without the world ending. Neither did we witness the demise of the stock market. As the new century unfolded, a solicitation showed up in my mail from Fidelity Investments to accept some free online trades should I choose to open an account. Accountants never reject anything free. So there I went again. Out of the CDs came a good portion of my savings (what I had accumulated since earlier losses).

This time was going to be different, or so I thought. I intended to be more selective this time. Surely some tech stocks that had declined significantly from the bursting of the dot-com bubble (most tech stock prices peaked in March 2000) would have to be buys now. Tech-stock prices fell dramatically over a short period of time. During 2001, many of these tech stocks had fallen in price well over 50 percent from their highs of the previous year. I decided to go with a few big tech names, familiar to anyone who followed technology stocks. This time, I not only made sure that future expected earnings justified my buying, but also that the company balance sheets reflected the financial flexibility to generate the expected earnings. That is, I made sure the companies' balance sheets did not reflect much debt but did reflect plenty of liquid (cash or near-cash) assets. I wanted to know that the companies had the financial wherewithal to carry on business operations at a level of their predicted profitability.

My free trades soon got used, and the tech stocks I bought went down—and then down some more. My risk-assessment technique was still not right since my outcome revealed that I had bought stocks at prices that left me vulnerable to significant stock-price declines. I still did not know how to buy low.

I started talking to myself. "Paul, you have been teaching accounting courses, and sometimes finance courses, for years." My teaching career had started in 1985 at Tulane University College in New Orleans, Louisiana, when I was teaching with my master of business administration (MBA) and certified public accountant (CPA) under my belt. This was well before I concluded my doctor of business administration (DBA) in accounting in 1994. So, by 2000, I had been teaching students for fifteen years how to create the information that goes into corporate financial statements. Surely I must understand how to use this information toward successful investing!

I continued with my little talk. "Paul, you have the basis for analyzing the financials and should be able to come up with a disciplined, commonsense approach to investing. You have got to learn what it means to buy low. That way, no matter how the story goes, you got in real low from the beginning and should face minimal downside risk."

That's exactly what I did. I learned how to buy low.

Developing the Balance-Sheet Strategy

My miserable start to investing eventually led me to put my accounting knowledge to practical, commonsense use. I came to realize that speculating on future expected earnings as a primary basis for buying low was far too arbitrary. There had to be a basis for protecting against the possibility that expected earnings would fail to materialize. There had to be a substantive basis for establishing a low stock price number at which buying there or below would eliminate most risk associated with a potential failure of expected profits. I finally learned that there is a lot more to the balance sheet of a company relative to determining a low price than I had ever imagined. By now it was almost 2003.

In 2003, I developed my balance-sheet strategy for buying common stocks. It is this balance-sheet buying strategy that explains my unusually high stock returns since early 2003, and it is this formula I will share in this book.

I've honed my balance-sheet buying strategy since 2003 and feel a very natural sense about it today. While my buying habits may be similar to those of others who have written books on various aspects of investing, the buying practice I currently follow is unique in that it is strictly the by-product of learning critical investing concepts as a result of my early self-inflicted investment mistakes. That is, through my own unique set of mistakes, I learned what intuitively should work when it comes to identifying a low stock price, and then I converted that intuition into a successful, practical, personalized buying strategy.

To be successful on your own with investing in common stocks, I'm convinced your approach has to make practical sense to you so that you are able to implement your strategy properly. That is, the understanding cannot be in another's mind—it has to be in your mind. I want to communicate my formula with you because it has worked so well for me, and I want to communicate it in a manner you can replicate. If you choose to apply it, keep in mind that it will take time and effort to achieve your comfort zone.

You may want to modify different parts of my formula as you become more comfortable with using the balance sheet to practice lower-the-risk buying. When it comes to how much risk we are willing to assume, each person is different. I try to buy quality stocks when they are deeply underpriced, and as I present the specific parts of my formula through this book, you will detect how extremely risk averse I am when it comes to buying low.

Simply put, I buy stocks primarily based on the balance sheet. I do take into account expected earnings, but do not use earnings as the centrality of my approach to buying stocks. The personal success I detailed in the introduction chapter to this book, in the form of my annualized portfolio returns, is attributed to my balance-sheet buying strategy. The money left from the tech stocks, which I sold at a loss before 2003, was redistributed to other stocks that satisfied my newfound, buy-low, balance-sheet-based investment approach.

Since implementing the balance-sheet buying strategy in early 2003, my portfolio resources have been redistributed from time to time to new stocks as appropriate. However, I'm generally redistributing (selling stocks and buying others) money that has grown through significant realized gains. As already stated, the money multiplied more than twenty-six times during the ten years since the inception of my strategy.

To outperform, you must avoid buying cheap (poor) stocks and consistently buy good stocks at dirt-cheap prices. The latter are always readily available, by the way. You just have to consistently find the best ones via a method that works. This book will help you become a better "fisherman" when it comes to locating the best common stocks to buy. Chapter 10 illustrates how to fish, or screen, for valuable stocks from the vast population of stocks. Chapter 11 uses a real present-day company to illustrate the formula process I go through to identify a low price for the company.

> **To outperform, you must avoid buying cheap (poor) stocks and consistently buy good stocks at dirt-cheap prices.**

Most likely, the readers of this book include a good number of investors who can relate to the personal experiences I shared in this chapter. You have been through some bad investing experiences but have gotten better as a result. During my first two ventures into the stock market, I lost money because I didn't buy the right stocks at the right prices. I approached investing without a heightened sense of responsibility for knowing the level of risk being taken. After I lost money on my first two ventures into stock investing, I believe God helped me develop an approach to buying stocks that is consistent with practicing good stewardship over financial resources. Since I learned to—more often than not—buy solid stocks at the right prices, returns have greatly exceeded broad market results.

Learn Balance-Sheet Analysis or Lose the Money

This second chapter is titled "Learn It or Lose It." The first *it* in the title refers to the statement of financial position of a corporation whose ownership interests are traded in the form of common stock over a public stock exchange overseen by the Securities and Exchange Commission (SEC). That statement is called the balance sheet. The words *learn it* mean learning to read and analyze the balance sheet. The second *it* refers to the money that will be lost if the balance sheet does not become central to the risk-assessment habits of one who buys common stocks.

So if you don't learn how to read the balance sheet, you can't assess how low the price really is. Thus, you are left to other devices—all of which are less substantive—to determine when to buy. For example, many buy and sell stocks strictly based on interpreting stock-chart patterns. Stock charts are pictures that reflect stock-price trends, indicative of investors' past sentiment toward a stock. I have nothing against stock charts, and they can complement the overall due diligence activities one performs before making an investment. In fact, when I'm buying low, I fully expect the chart to look terrible—that's the way it looks when you buy a stock near its bottom. However, value that is real cannot be discerned from a picture alone. The balance sheet can, by itself, communicate a great deal about value, though, and help you discern whether the current stock price is truly low or vulnerable to heading much lower still.

The balance sheet is a statement that reflects a company's current financial standing. It reflects all past transaction activity of the company since its origin. That is, it reflects the accumulated worth of the company to date. It excludes expectations with regard to future profits or losses the company might or might not experience. Using a proper balance-sheet analysis approach, one can determine the likely floor price for a given stock.

Of course, this book, as with any book, cannot suggest a formula that is guaranteed to work every time or produce above-average returns. However, proper assessment of the balance sheet is the critical feature of risk assessment under my lower-the-risk buying approach. Earnings are extracted from another accounting-based report, namely the income statement, a financial report that covers a limited time period and focuses on the recent operations of the company. While earnings and earnings projections are useful in determining the relationship between the current stock price and its reward potential, the balance sheet is the only statement that can tell us where the floor stock price may be, should earnings expectations prove too high and lead to disappointment among investors.

> While earnings and earnings projections are useful in determining the relationship between the current stock price and its reward potential, the balance sheet is the only statement that can tell us where the floor stock price may be, should earnings expectations prove too high and lead to disappointment among investors.

Money can definitely be made in certain market eras by purchasing high-flying stocks experiencing significant earnings growth, but a lot of money can also be lost if those earnings slow. That kind of buying is not what I advocate in this book. Many semiconductors, telecoms, and other tech stocks reached incredibly lofty stock prices into the spring of 2000, and many investors were still buying. Also, some of those stocks fell over 90 percent in price over the next year or so, once the momentum buying stopped. An overly optimistic earnings-growth buying frenzy had moved stocks to unrealistic prices above their balance-sheet floor prices.

Buying close to the balance-sheet floor value, as will be explained in this book, protects an investor from the fallout associated with earnings optimism that turns into earnings pessimism. This type of earnings fallout is the principle explanation behind most large investment losses. You must consistently buy low to avoid subjecting yourself to investment losses that result from an earnings fallout. No person can know for certain whether future earnings will be poor, good, or excellent. However, anyone can know what a company is approximately worth today, aside from future events, by properly assessing the balance sheet.

Finding—via balance-sheet analysis—and buying deep-value stocks for which earnings expectations are decent to strong produces a value-growth situation in which a lot of money can be made without taking on significant risk. These scenarios represent ideal buying situations.

Since I developed my own successful approach to buying stocks and implemented it in early 2003, I have followed it carefully, especially during the major market downturn of 2008 and 2009 when many people thought another Great Depression was imminent. I find it logical that my method continues to work because it is based on commonsense analysis and eliminates emotion-based decision making, which can destroy any portfolio.

My miserable investing start brought me to a place where my extensive educational background in accounting, and to a somewhat lesser degree in finance, has now translated into a practical, simple-to-apply, and highly successful stock-buying methodology that I can share in this book. Valuing stocks for possible investments has become second nature to me now. I want you to develop this second nature. As with anything that becomes second nature, you must practice it over and over again. So it will take some effort on your part to really understand the moving parts of the strategic formula presented—although the formula itself, as revealed in chapter 11, is ready to go and easy to apply. I will explain the moving parts too. The potential rewards more than justify the effort involved, based on my investment returns.

> Valuing stocks for possible investments has become second nature to me now. I want you to develop this second nature.

How This Book Is Organized

In chapter 3 I will begin to address the balance sheet, starting with an overall view of the balance sheet as an integral part of a set of financial statements.

Chapter 4 continues the discussion of the balance sheet by explaining how it can be broken down to help an investor determine when a stock is looking like a potential buy.

Chapters 5 and 6 present a series of examples using hypothetical balance sheets to help ascertain what I refer to as an *initial floor price*.

Chapter 7 discusses the coupling of market expectations of a company's future earnings with the *initial floor price* derived from balance-sheet assessment to find what I call my *adjusted floor price*, a price I'm willing pay for a stock.

Chapter 8 discusses my balance-sheet buying strategy with regard to identifying small companies that can offer outstanding value at times due to, among other things, the absence of broad analyst coverage typically present with large corporations. It will discuss a few of my best stock success stories and a couple of my worst ones since I began implementing my balance-sheet buying strategy in 2003.

Chapter 9 presents a checklist of some things I've learned, from my personal investing experiences, to always consider before buying a stock. This checklist represents qualitative factors that describe my core investing philosophy. While not exhaustive, the list can help you both avoid and reduce potential losses and, conversely, realize stronger gains.

In chapter 10, I'll discuss how to screen the universe of stocks into a much smaller investing pool that can be analyzed for potential purchase candidates. I'll take you online to a website where we will filter the total universe of stocks trading over major US exchanges into a much-reduced pool that includes only stocks that meet specified criteria consistent with my balance-sheet approach to buying low.

In Chapter 11, we will remain online to analyze an actual company stock for the purpose of determining a price I would be willing to pay for a share. Chapter 11 also includes a worksheet I call the Adjusted Floor Price Scorecard, which you can use as a template for applying

The Adjusted Floor Price Scorecard is the formula.

my balance-sheet buying formula to any given stock you choose to analyze. The output of the Adjusted Floor Price Scorecard is the *adjusted floor price*, the price at which the stock may become a buy. The Adjusted Floor Price Scorecard is the formula. You can visit my website at www.choosestockswisely.com to gain access to my Adjusted Floor Price Scorecard as a spreadsheet tool. I'll give more specifics, later, on accessing the scorecard at the website. I also show how the worksheet formula is completed manually in chapter 11.

Chapter 12 addresses the subject of what constitutes a reasonable percentage of one's total investment portfolio to put into common stocks that satisfy my balance-sheet buying strategy.

In chapter 13, I share the most important investment I made in life—namely, placing my faith in Jesus Christ. Sharing my faith gives meaning to why I wanted to share my buying methodology with you in this book.

Chapter 14, the final chapter, presents questions and answers intended to clarify certain concepts throughout the book—important concepts that need to be understood for my buying methodology to be used in the proper context. You may observe that some themes in chapter 14 were mentioned in earlier chapters. Any repetition is intentional, for the purpose of careful clarification of concepts that are critically important to the proper application of my buying methodology.

Chapters 5, 6, 10, and 11 are the hands-on, how-to chapters in this book. I hope, after reading the entire book, you will find it a continual investing resource and that these four chapters will be particularly useful to you time and time again.

Conclusion

The common denominator in identifying underpriced common stocks, regardless of company size, is proper analysis of the balance sheet. Learning how to use the balance sheet when buying common stocks will provide a substantive basis for believing a stock is low and therefore a buy. The balance sheet provides the proper context for observing recent earnings performance and the earnings outlook.

Buying because you have a good feeling about the future performance of a company will end up costing you a bundle if you do it enough times. Perhaps you have already been down that road. I had to travel that wrong road twice before I took the correct road of buying stocks based on proper balance-sheet assessment.

CHAPTER 3

LEARN IT: "IT" IS THE BALANCE SHEET

The stock market is filled with individuals who know the price of everything, but the value of nothing.[1]
—Philip Fisher

Philip Fisher is known as a pioneer *growth* investor, but his words in the above quote imply that knowing how to value a stock is essential to investing. That is, you don't have to be identified as a *value* investor to realize that an ability to identify value is critical to success in the stock market. Over my years of investing, I've participated in online stock message board or chat board conversations. Among messages that offer little to chew on are well-thought-out messages written by certain posters I've come to know as experienced value-based investors. These posters tend to focus on fundamental valuation issues rather than momentary emotions. Again, there are other posters who offer little substance and whose posts evidence a practice of going along with the momentary, fickle mood swings of the market. To

---

[1] See "The Top 17 Investment Quotes of All Time" at www.investopedia.com

make money in the stock market over the longer term, you must remain emotionally detached and know how to discern value.

Present sentiment is a powerful influence on stock prices in the shorter term, for sure. If you want to buy a good stock at a low price, you must expect that the stock is not trading as though it is in favor with investors. Thus, to buy low it is important to always separate emotion from the investing decision. That is harder than it sounds because none of us "feel" easy about going against the market trend. It makes us wonder if there is something wrong with us when the vast majority disagrees with our thinking. It tempts us to question our reasoning. In my view, the only way to buy the common stock of solid companies near the bottom is to be a staunch contrarian. Fisher's quote implies that the market's herd mentality is going to provide opportunities to the one who recognizes real value.

What is a contrarian, though? In the context of buying common stocks at low prices, a true contrarian is not simply one who runs contrary to the current market direction on a stock; that person may be running right off a cliff, since the crowd may be justified at times in their actions toward a stock. It is more than that. A true contrarian in the stock market is one who knows how to value a common stock and is willing to differ with the crowd when the crowd has mispriced the stock relative to its value.

So how can we know when we are buying value? What are you going to read here that is different from what you have read before about buying common stocks? The case I make, backed by results that have outpaced market indices by a wide margin, is that the financial statements have to be used in the context of the information they are intended to provide.

3   Three primary financial statements are required to be produced by management of corporations whose stocks are traded over a public exchange overseen by the SEC. These statements must be prepared in compliance with generally accepted accounting principles (GAAP). The statements are the balance sheet, the income statement, and the statement of cash flows.

This book focuses on the balance sheet as the essential financial accounting report for risk assessment in identifying solid common stocks trading at low prices. To provide proper context, though, an overall perspective of the full set of financial statements is important. Each financial report has a distinctive purpose, and that purpose must be understood for the information it offers to be applied properly in the valuation of a common stock.

When trying to identify a solid company selling at a low price, you have to focus on risk assessment. Risk is the downside, whereas reward is the upside. If I invest a thousand dollars in a stock, I am not referring to risk if I say, "I think this stock could go up fifty percent this year." I am referring to risk if I say, "This stock could drop fifty percent." My goal is to avoid buying stocks with anything but minor risks. That is, I want the market to have beaten the risk out of the price before I take my position. If you learn how to properly assess a stock's value, you will not always buy the bottom, but you will have much more confidence that you are buying low.

> My goal is to avoid buying stocks with anything but minor risks. That is, I want the market to have beaten the risk out of the price before I take my position.

By the way, the market provides plenty of opportunities to buy low. So anxiousness has no place when it comes to successfully buying common stocks. It's unwise to commit to something until you understand the costs of that commitment. In fact, the cost may well be worth it, but your analysis of the situation is how you discern that the cost is justified. Getting in over your head by buying stocks without really understanding the reasons for your buying decisions can happen faster than you might think.

Let's consider the financial statements in terms of what they communicate to investors. Accounting (financial) statements exist to help the investment community assess the level of risk (potential downside) relative to the level of reward (potential upside) on an investment.

Let's start with the balance sheet, also known as the statement of financial position. This all-encompassing statement tells us about the financial health of the company. It is indeed a statement of position, or a status report. It gives the accounting value of a common stock at a point in time that is the result of all accounting debits and credits recorded since the company's beginning. In its heading, a balance sheet is often dated with the words *as of* the closing date of an accounting period. The words *as of* emphasize that the report is not a periodic report on performance, but rather a report that includes the entire history of financial activity from the company's beginning.

The recorded worth of all the common stock shares a company has in the marketplace—shares usually referred to as outstanding shares—is shown on the balance sheet. Relative to conducting risk assessment before buying a common stock, how can I overstate the significance of the balance sheet, given that it shows the accounting value of a company's common stock at a point in time? After all, a stock is purchased at a point in time, and the only way to minimize the risk of losing money on a stock investment is to avoid paying more for the stock than it is worth at the time of purchase. Since the balance sheet is the only financial statement that *is* a statement of a company's present financial worth, how can it not be the focal financial statement of one's risk analysis relative to buying stocks?

> **Relative to conducting risk assessment before buying a common stock, how can I overstate the significance of the balance sheet, given that it shows the accounting value of a company's common stock at a point in time?**

The financial worth of a company is regarded as equity on a balance sheet. Equity refers to ownership. Where ownership is held in the form of common stock shares, as is the case with publicly-traded corporations, the balance-sheet equity is referred to as stockholders' equity. In addition to stockholders' equity, the balance sheet also shows the details of a company's assets and liabilities. The asset and liability accounts help explain the nature of stockholders' equity. The assets reflect the resources the company has to work with, and the liabilities reflect the obligations that must be satisfied from the assets. The excess of the assets over liabilities is equal to the stockholders' equity that belongs to the shareholders.

The balance-sheet model is as follows:

Assets = Liabilities + Equity

This simple algebraic equation can be restated as:

Assets − Liabilities = Equity

Again, the total stockholders' equity shown on the balance sheet of a publicly traded corporation is the residual accounting number after liabilities are subtracted from assets and is indicative of the accounting value of stockholder interest in the company at the date of the balance sheet. Remember that this statement is *not* a recent performance report, but rather reflects the company's financial position, inclusive of the entire performance history of the company from inception to the balance-sheet date. Again, this statement reflects the financial condition of the business at a point in time. It is a snapshot of the company, financially speaking. An investor uses the balance sheet to determine how much worth has been logged in to date (i.e., stockholders' equity) and what the composition of that worth looks like (i.e., assets and liabilities).

Two different companies can have exactly the same amount of stockholders' equity and the same number of outstanding common stock shares such that the stockholders' equity per share (Stockholders' Equity / # of Shares Outstanding = Stockholders' Equity per Share) for both companies is exactly the same. Note that stockholders' equity per share is the same thing as book value per share. While the book value per share of the two companies may be equal, the quality of the stockholders' equity can be radically different, such that one company is much stronger than the other in terms of its financial flexibility not only to survive but also to realize future growth via earnings performance.

Thus, all equity balances are not created equal. Chapters 5 and 6 will illustrate this truth. By studying the composition of the balance sheet stockholders' equity, as detailed through asset and liability accounts, you can discern the quality of the stockholders' equity. In fact, the quality of the stockholders' equity *must* be understood to assess risk properly and have success in both identifying quality businesses and buying into them at low prices. Your goal in buying common stocks is to buy quality at a low price. If you want

> **Your goal in buying common stocks is to buy quality at a low price.**

to buy the common stock of good companies at a low price, never underestimate the power of the balance sheet to help you do that.

So let's review—what does a balance sheet reveal? It reveals the financial position of a company at a point in time. It gives us the book value of the company through the stated amount of the stockholders' equity. It reveals the quality of this book value through a breakout of the value into asset and liability account balances. It is not an activity report. It is a status report. In assessing risk, I want to buy low. To buy low, I have to be able to determine what my position is worth today, without regard to future performance. The future is uncertain, but the present is known. I need to know where the floor value is when I buy because I don't want to buy above that floor.

Of the set of a company's financials (balance sheet, income statement, statement of cash flows), the balance sheet is the only statement that tells me where the company stands right now. It is therefore the report I need to focus on when buying stocks. The balance sheet is uniquely suited for helping me avoid facing substantial risk when purchasing stocks. My portfolio returns strongly validate that my balance-sheet strategy for making low-risk purchases of common stocks is highly effective.

What about the other two financial statements that complete a set of GAAP financials? Well, both the income (earnings) statement and the statement of cash flows are activity reports. Neither report on the financial position of the company, which the balance sheet does. They are not dated "as of" the closing date as the balance sheet is; they are dated with language such as "for the period ending" at the closing date.

The income statement reports on recent earnings performance for the most recent accounting period; it is either a quarterly or annual report. The statement of cash flows reflects the sources and uses of cash, also for the most recent accounting period. Basically, these two activity reports—the income statement and the statement of cash flows—detail activity that occurred during the latest accounting period that caused the balance-sheet position to change during that period. That is, these reports help us understand what is happening to the balance sheet period by period. Their purpose, then, only solidifies the fact that the balance sheet is the key report for an investor to understand before investing in any company. In other words, the two short-term activity reports—namely, the income statement and the statement of cash flows—exist for the sole purpose of explaining recent changes to a company's financial position captured in the balance sheet.

Again, since the balance sheet is not merely a periodic activity report covering a short time span like the other two statements but is rather an all-encompassing status report, we can understand that all financial performance activity from the advent of the business is depicted in the composition of the existing asset and liability accounts on the most recently published balance sheet. All prior financial successes and failures are there. If you want to buy low, you have to conclude where the floor or bottom potential stock price could be. You cannot determine that without proper assessment of the balance sheet. It is the only statement that communicates the financial position of a company.

Commonsense risk avoidance suggests that I don't want to pay more than the present worth of a stock. I want to focus on what is known at the current time to avoid facing the potential losses related to not knowing about the future. Thus, understanding the company's present worth, as depicted by the balance sheet, is critical before buying any stock. This does not mean I disregard the future performance expectations altogether when buying stocks. However, future performance expectations are a secondary consideration, whereas the balance sheet is the primary driver relative to where I am willing to buy a common stock.

Under my balance-sheet buying strategy, proper analysis of the most recent balance sheet alone gives me an _initial floor price_, which completely excludes future performance expectations. Once I derive this _initial floor price_ from the balance-sheet analysis, I will then consider any available future earnings performance expectations and, if warranted, make an adjustment to the _initial floor price_. After adjustment, I refer to the price as an _adjusted floor price_. I will consider buying a stock at this price or less. Before this book is completed, you will see my strategy applied step-by-step.

Empirical evidence shows that future stock prices are driven by future earnings performance, but nothing in that evidence shows that you can consistently make above-average returns and conversely avoid big losses by adhering to an earnings-based strategy of buying common stocks. Saying that future stock prices depend on earnings performance is equivalent to saying stock-price reward, or upside, potential depends on earnings performance. I don't disagree with that. In fact, it is the very truth that future stock prices depend on future earnings performance that makes buying stocks based on future earnings expectations so dangerous. Yet most market participants practice just that kind of buying strategy today.

I learned the hard way from my early investing days that if you buy primarily based on future expected earnings—that is, if you follow an earnings-based buying strategy—you'd better hope the expected earnings are achieved or exceeded. I suffered significant investment losses in my earliest ventures into common stocks due to buying based, in large measure, on earnings expectations. When expectations were not met, I had no substantive basis for knowing how far or fast the stock price could decline.

I also learned that if you buy strictly based on earnings, you will never be comfortable with a buy-and-hold strategy. You will always be thinking about selling before every earnings report and will find yourself living from one earnings report to the next. That is, you will feel compelled to follow your stock holdings very closely and will probably find yourself actively trading stocks, whether you want to or not. I know now that when I buy quality stocks that are really low priced—meaning the stocks are not highly dependent on future earnings expectations—based on my balance-sheet strategy to buying low-risk stocks, I can usually hold my positions comfortably until the company realizes the kind of performance to drive the stock prices much higher. Buying at a price that has the risk beaten out of the price gives you greater confidence with regard to holding your position until it pays off.

My position is that the best buying strategy is one that protects you from buying at prices that make you overly dependent on how the company actually performs after you buy. Buying low must primarily focus then on proper risk assessment, not proper reward assessment. To buy low, you must buy when the stock price has been pushed low enough to have already compensated for any risk related to the possible negative outcome of future company earnings performance falling short of what is expected. Determining that stock price level is impossible without properly assessing the only financial report that can get you there—the balance sheet.

If you overpay for the stock based on lofty earnings expectations without giving proper context to those earnings expectations by evaluating the balance sheet, and the positive earnings projections fail to materialize, you will, unfortunately, only find out that you overpaid after it is already too late. The market reacts to earnings news efficiently—meaning instantly.

Positive earnings, once reported in the income statement, are added to the stockholders' equity of the balance sheet. Negative earnings have the opposite impact on stockholders' equity. Without question, then, earnings are important to how much reward a stockholder may realize through an improving stock price. The reason a share of stock can become worth more is because stockholders' equity on the balance sheet will be increased through positive earnings performance.

Let's recap. While earnings drive future stock prices and therefore earnings forecasts help determine reward potential, projected earnings do not serve as a sound basis for risk assessment that serves to determine a low buying price on a common stock. Anyone who uses earnings in a context other than intended is likely to be counting his/her losses soon. If you want to buy a common stock, study the balance sheet's stockholders' equity (see chapters 5 and 6 for illustrations) to determine a floor price to avoid taking unwarranted risk. In any given market, undervalued stocks will be available to buy. The key to consistently making money in stocks is through patiently choosing the best stock candidates for purchase. You must buy good stocks while they are "on sale."

I believe the widespread lack of familiarity with balance-sheet assessment has led to a flawed notion that the balance sheet is mostly irrelevant to stock valuation—for buying or selling stocks—and that earnings analysis alone is sufficient for identifying buying or selling points with stocks. Further, I believe this flawed notion costs investors plenty through real losses and reduced positive returns stemming from buying the wrong stocks or buying at entry levels that are too high—or impatiently selling out of stock holdings where price recovery is warranted.

The use of the balance sheet as the primary financial report for proper risk assessment makes the art of buying good stocks at low prices probable. My personal portfolio returns—derived from following a balance-sheet-based buying strategy—support my perspective that a lack of balance-sheet emphasis in the market leads to anomalous prices in the short term, thereby creating the opportunity for abnormally high returns to accrue to the one who learns how to properly assess the balance sheet before buying common stocks. That is, investors who don't give proper attention to the balance sheet may actually be the ones who create the opportunity for a balance-sheet investor to buy at an artificially low price, because market participants who disregard the balance sheet are likely the ones who sell their positions at the wrong times, out of impatience, fear, or frustration at bargain basement prices.

Buy low and sell high is a practical, commonsense approach to investing. Many market participants, however, believe it is impossible to practically apply a buy-low, sell-high strategy. If buying low is impossible to apply, then there is no meaning or purpose for the admonition to buy low—and buying stocks would indeed be akin to gambling.

My performance results prove buying low is possible. Buying low must be properly defined and then applied in an absolute sense, just as selling high must be. As stated early on and repeated several times, this book is not about how to sell high but presents my balance-sheet strategy for buying low. It has been my balance-sheet strategy for making low-risk buys that explains my strong investment returns—much more so than my success at selling high. Even though I typically end up selling below the highs—often well below the highs—I rarely overpay for a stock. Buying low has allowed me to realize significant investment returns, even though I frequently miss selling at the highs.

Statistical hypotheses, or notions of what might be true, can be tested and either accepted as true or rejected as false. Mistakes can be made, though. There are two error types that can occur: a type 1 error and a type 2 error, the latter being much more serious. A type 1 error means rejecting a hypothesis as false when it is actually true. A type 2 error means accepting a hypothesis as true when it is actually false. Apply this to buying common stocks. Which of the following is the more serious mistake: not buying a stock that should have been bought (type 1 error) or buying one that should have been rejected (type 2 error)? The latter situation is worse, of course. Not buying a stock that would have worked out means missing out on gains, but no money was lost. Buying a stock that subsequently remains under the price you paid means losing money. In investing, you want to avoid the type 2 error. Using the balance sheet to identify good stocks at low prices is the best way to avoid committing type 2 errors and thereby significantly improve the chances of making money on stocks you buy.

Earnings will become more important after you buy low, since earnings will define your reward and help determine your selling point. However, when you buy based on the balance sheet, you are far less dependent on the actual realization of earnings forecasts to avoid loss of invested capital. Every stock you choose may not realize large gains, but some probably will, and it does not take many of these big gainers to produce strong overall portfolio returns. Minimizing losses through a disciplined balance-sheet buying strategy can improve your overall performance radically. Using my balance-sheet strategy to buy low-risk stocks is *the* significant factor behind my average annualized return of almost 39 percent since I started using the approach in early 2003.

CHAPTER 4

BREAKING DOWN THE BALANCE SHEET

Wealth gained by dishonesty will be diminished. But he who gathers by labor will increase.
—Proverbs 13:11 (New King James Version)

Stockholders' equity represents stockholder wealth; in other words, equity is wealth. The balance sheet is where you will find stockholders' equity, along with the asset and liability components that result in that equity figure. Said another way, the balance sheet is a statement of company wealth and includes the composition of that wealth.

In the college-level business finance course often referred to as "financial management," any textbook will state, typically on the first page of the first chapter, that the goal of financial management should be to maximize stockholder wealth rather than to maximize profit. The person in the corporation primarily responsible for managing the finances of the company for the shareholders' benefit is the chief financial officer (CFO).

Profit, or earnings, is derived from recent operating activity and depicted on the income statement. Wealth is derived from the entirety of financial activity since a company's origin and is depicted on the balance sheet in the Stockholder Equity section. Again, the CFO's job is to maximize stockholder wealth. To illustrate why maximization of short-term profits is not always consistent with the maximization of long-term wealth, consider the following example. A textile company seeks to increase its periodic profits by dumping dangerous toxins into a nearby river, thereby reducing the costs it would have otherwise encountered had it eliminated the toxins in a socially responsible manner. This seems to work out well for a couple of years. The toxins contaminate the river, though, and this inevitably brings a lot of negative attention to the company. The bad publicity leads to the company's customers leaving in droves. Additionally, legal costs skyrocket, and before long the company is forced to file for bankruptcy protection. A shortsighted emphasis on short-term profitability can be a costly thing to stockholder wealth.

So emphasizing wealth (long-term prosperity) over profit (short-term prosperity) is the sound and ethical approach. Executive management should lend support to the company's CFO as he or she seeks to manage the application of company assets in an optimal manner for the maximization of stockholders' equity over the long term, as opposed to managing for optimal earnings per share (EPS) in the near term. Unfortunately, too many investors today lack the patience for wealth building and alternatively prefer to get rich quick, often putting pressure on corporate management to do whatever it takes to get the earnings up now.

You will best protect against loss of your invested capital and conversely realize better returns by investing in companies that manage shareholder value for the long term. Further, remember that a company's long-term worth is found on the balance sheet, and that worth is labeled as stockholders' equity. You want a company CFO who manages the company's balance sheet

You will best protect against loss of your invested capital and conversely realize better returns by investing in companies that manage shareholder value for the long term.

in a responsible manner, behaving as a steward of the stockholders' interest over the long term. The only way to know whether your interest is being managed for the long term is through—you guessed it—proper assessment of the balance sheet.

Making money on an investment is as appealing to me as the next person. However, I would rather wait on my sought-after return than benefit from any kind of get-rich-quick scheme. As the scripture verse at the start of this chapter directs, the momentary rewards of illicit gains will be lost anyway—and lost in many different senses of the word, in my view. You cannot buy peace of mind with money.

When it comes to stock investments, you want to invest in companies that evidence—through their balance sheets—the stewardship commitment of CFOs to the management of company finances in a manner that supports stockholders' long-term interests. A CFO with this kind of commitment is not going to be careless with company resources—that is, not a spendthrift, not one to take on excessive debt, not one comfortable with company resources being dedicated to overly risky ventures, and the like. The balance sheet tells a story about the CFO. You can tell whether a company has been managed well financially to date by analyzing the most recent balance sheet.

It is hard to overstate the implications of investing in a company without balance-sheet evidence of a good money manager at the helm in the CFO role. Before I entrust my hard-earned money, through purchase of common stock, to a corporation to use as it sees fit, knowing a lot about the CFO is important. I want the CFO to be an effective and frugal money manager, one who is an excellent steward acting on behalf of the owners. While the balance sheet reflects the totality of management performance to date, it also paints a picture of the CFO's money management style, assuming the CFO has been with the company for more than a couple of years or so. Of course, if the CFO just arrived, researching his/her history would be important before considering a financial stake in the company. The personal integrity of the CFO is essential to the welfare of your invested capital!

Recall that the balance sheet is a statement of wealth. The CFO is assigned the duty of attempting to maximize that wealth through effective asset management. The CFO does not market the company's products and thereby have a direct role in revenue generation, but this person has everything to do with the company's financial flexibility, which is accomplished by efficiently managing the balance sheet on behalf of the company stockholders (owners). So, again, the balance sheet reflects much about the money-management capabilities of the CFO.

Proper balance-sheet assessment enables you to ascertain the two most critical components of valuation. First, is the company financially solid? In chapter 5, I'll explain how this question is answered by introducing two balance-sheet quality standards that are part of my balance-sheet buying strategy. A solid balance sheet generally suggests that there's a good CFO behind that financial strength. Again, why would you entrust your money to anyone who is not an excellent financial manager? You want to see a strong balance sheet before you invest. Second, what is the approximate worth of the stockholders' equity? In chapters 5 and 6, I will illustrate, using eight hypothetical balance sheet examples, how to determine the approximate worth of the stockholders' equity and translate this worth into my *initial floor price* per share.

So balance-sheet assessment will not only tell us whether the stockholders' equity reflects quality but also give us an approximate worth of the balance sheet's stockholders' equity. This approximate worth gives us an *initial floor price*, which is a major step toward determining a low price for the stock.

This book has not yet illustrated the use of the balance sheet but has rather presented the *role* of the balance sheet during an investor's research efforts toward identifying quality stocks trading at low prices. In my view, theory always precedes practice. Jumping into practical application without sufficient theoretical basis is dangerous!

Let's take a look at a generic balance sheet and break it down into its key elements: assets, liabilities, and equity.

Balance Sheet
XYZ Company
As of December 31, 20xx

ASSETS   LIABILITIES

Current Assets: Current Liabilities
    Cash $ Accounts Payable $

Cash	$		Accounts Payable	$
Accounts Receivable	$		Accrued Liabilities	$
Inventory	$		Short term Debt	$
Total Current Assets	$		Total Current Liabilities	$
Noncurrent Assets:			Noncurrent Liabilities:	
Property, Plant, Equip.	$		Long term Debt	$
Goodwill	$		Total Liabilities	$
TOTAL ASSETS	$			
			STOCKHOLDERS' EQUITY	$
			TOTAL LIAB & ST. EQUITY	$

Recall the basic balance sheet accounting model that:

Assets = Liabilities + Equity;

Thus,

Assets – Liabilities = Equity

The purpose of this book is not to explain accounting; therefore, I will attempt to avoid technical language as much as possible. Instead, my aim is to write in terms that show the balance sheet a tremendously useful tool when analyzing common stocks for potential purchase. Note that the above balance sheet does not reflect all possible individual asset and liability accounts a balance sheet could include. It does, however, reflect accounts that are commonly found on balance sheets.

Think of assets as the company's resources that are available to help it make money. Think of liabilities as creditor claims against the assets. The unclaimed assets at any given point in time represent the resources that belong to the stockholders, known as the stockholders' equity. Since equity is the excess of assets over liabilities, it follows that the quality of the equity depends on the composition of the assets and liabilities. Equity may be described as "net assets," "net worth," or "book value." When equity is described as "stockholders' equity," the business is of corporate form, in which the equity belongs to stockholders.

The assets on a balance sheet are broken out between current assets and noncurrent assets. Here are a few things you should know about the balance sheet.

- Current assets are more liquid than noncurrent assets; that is, they are cash or closer to being converted into cash than are the noncurrent assets.
- Current assets are resources that can derive economic benefits (i.e., can generate revenue) for the shareholders for up to a year, loosely speaking, whereas noncurrent assets can derive economic benefits for the shareholders for more than a year.
- Current liabilities are creditor-based claims to company assets that must be satisfied from the assets within a year, whereas noncurrent liabilities have settlement dates of more than a year out.

Overall, a balance sheet orders assets and liabilities within a context of liquidation. Assets are listed from most liquid, starting with cash, to least liquid: for example, goodwill is a far less liquid asset than is the cash asset, so it is generally shown near the end of the assets listed on the balance sheet. Liabilities are listed from earliest (first) creditor claim on company assets to latest (last) creditor claim. Again, assets are ordered by liquidity, while liabilities are ordered by supremacy of claim to assets in liquidation.

Risk assessment by the balance sheet is the key to successful investing because it is the tool to identify good stocks trading at low prices. If you consistently buy quality stocks at low prices, your odds of consistently making money on your stock purchases are strong. Every stock may not become the next Apple or Google, but if you consistently buy good stocks at low prices, you don't have to find the next Apple or Google to generate returns on your portfolio that would be the envy of any investor. You don't have to be so preoccupied with quarterly earnings reports if you properly use the balance sheet to identify and buy good companies trading at low stock prices.

Don't get me wrong. You want to buy companies that you expect will be profitable in the future. However, the more important thing is to consistently buy quality at a low price—based on proper balance-sheet analysis—so that you are not dependent on future profitability to make good money.

Some will say this is just value-investing talk. Sure it is. But it is not focused on P/E (price-to-earnings, calculated as the stock price divided by the earnings per share) ratios in establishing the meaning of *value*. The P/E ratio is the predominant metric for gauging a stock's value in the stock market today. The denominator of any ratio is known as a base. Earnings per share (EPS) is the denominator of the P/E ratio, which means that value is earnings-based when one uses P/E to determine value. Most value investors try to implement a buy-low strategy by buying stocks when the P/E gets to a certain level—a level lower than the average P/E of the company's peers. A lower P/E means a lower stock price relative to the company's EPS.

Although the P/E is a useful ratio when analyzed in the appropriate context of the company's financial position (balance sheet), my successful buy-low strategy is a result of defining *value* primarily based on the balance sheet's described worth of stock-holders' equity—not based on periodic earnings. I want a lower price relative to the value of the company's stockholders' equity, as delineated by the asset and liability detail of the latest balance sheet. I have already defended my balance-sheet approach over an earnings approach in chapter 3 and will not do so here. Even so, the merits of my balance-sheet approach to buying will be explained carefully as you continue reading.

Can you imagine anyone who wants to consistently make money in the stock market not buying value? Does a so-called growth investor not care about value when buying common stocks? I can tell you, I like growth too, but I like it even more when I know I'm buying the growth potential at a dirt-cheap price. In fact, it has been in situations such as these where I've realized major returns.

Most investors have experienced the following at one time or other: You have a portfolio of stocks. While you may hit a home-run on one of them, you experience bad losses on several others that more than offset the big performer, causing your portfolio to perform poorly, even suffering net overall portfolio losses at times.

Not losing money on stocks is the best way to be assured of coming out ahead. You want a portfolio that excludes, or at least minimizes, losers. While the earnings report and not the balance sheet is the talk of the marketplace, reward can never be viewed in proper context without careful risk assessment. Earnings per share do not speak to whether the underlying balance sheet supports a stock price higher than the current price.

The balance sheet reflects critical risk assessment information that is vital for identifying quality stocks selling at low prices. A company's liquidity is revealed by its balance sheet. A company must have enough cash and noncash assets that can expeditiously be converted into cash to pay operating bills and to pay off debt in a timely manner. The balance sheet shows us the amount of intangible assets that factor into the stockholders' equity of the company. It is difficult to know the cash worth of an intangible. Therefore, the presence of intangible assets on a company balance sheet presents a valuation risk of its own. The balance sheet reveals to us how much financial leverage, or debt, the company employs in support of its assets.

Many readers are familiar with a financial ratio known as the current ratio. It is the ratio of current assets to current liabilities. These ratio components are found on the balance sheet. If, for example, the balance sheet shows that total current assets are $2 million and total current liabilities are $1 million, the current ratio would be calculated as $2M/$1M = 2:1, or simply, 2. The point of the ratio is to reveal how able the company is to pay off the obligations that will soon come due. So a current ratio of 2 would imply a company could settle its day-to-day bills twice over from its current assets. The greater the excess of current assets over current liabilities, as evidenced by a higher current ratio, the more liquidity for day-to-day operations of the company; this means imminent financial distress is less likely.

Clearly, liquidity is a critical element of risk assessment since a company could conceivably be making money hand over fist but have so much of its money tied up in longer-term assets (which cannot be easily converted into cash) that it comes face-to-face with technical bankruptcy. This actually occurs more than you might imagine. Only the balance sheet can reveal whether adequate liquidity exists to carry on day-to-day operations.

Certainly, issues such as what industry the company is part of will affect evaluation of risk. For example, a biotech company's latest balance sheet may reflect strong liquidity, yet its quarterly cash depletion rate—associated with developing and testing a potential drug not yet approved for commercial use—is so high that the liquidity picture is likely to deteriorate rapidly. So the balance sheet must be assessed within the context of the company's profile. The point, though, is that the balance sheet provides the core inputs for liquidity analysis, and liquidity analysis is fundamental to risk assessment.

Debt (financial leverage) is found on the balance sheet, usually under long-term liabilities. However, any portion that will mature within the next twelve months from the balance-sheet date will be reflected under current liabilities as short-term debt. Assessing the amount of financial leverage is another major element of risk assessment. All debt, both short-term and long-term, must be considered. The balance sheet tells the story.

Recall that stockholders' equity represents the balance sheet's stated worth of the common stock circulating in the marketplace. The more liquid the company, the lower the percentage of intangible assets to total assets, and the less obligated by debt, the greater the company's financial flexibility to take advantage of future opportunities and, accordingly, the higher the quality of stockholders' equity.

To buy low, and thereby avoid potentially significant investment losses, one must understand the balance sheet with regard to the accounting value of a share of common stock. One must learn how to assess the balance sheet's contents, namely its assets and liabilities, in order to determine the quality of the stockholders' equity and to derive a floor value per share (*initial floor price*) for a unit of stockholders' equity—namely a share of the company's common stock. Only then can one examine the current stock price on the market with any confidence. To buy low, you must have a balance-sheet basis for judging that the current stock price is low. After reading the next two chapters, I hope you will become much more comfortable using the balance sheet as a powerful tool for ascertaining value in a context of buying common stocks at low prices.

CHAPTER 5

THE BALANCE SHEET: WHEN EQUAL IS NOT EQUAL, PART I

Your scales and weights must be accurate.
—Leviticus 19: 36a (New Living Translation)

All balance sheets are not created equal; that's worth remembering. Relative to identifying stocks to buy, many investors almost exclusively rely on earnings analysis instead of placing the emphasis on balance-sheet analysis, as I'm advocating. How does one value a stock when there are zero earnings or when a slowdown in the economy leads to negative earnings (i.e., net losses)? Do we automatically conclude the stock worthless?

The only way to use earnings to determine whether a stock is trading below its fair value, and therefore a good buy, is to consider earnings in the context of what the balance sheet is presently worth. There is a general lack of familiarity with balance-sheet analysis among many market participants, and the balance sheet is often largely disregarded. The balance sheet

is the centerpiece of my buying strategy. If you learn how to use the balance
sheet, it will make you a much stronger
market participant.

> **The balance sheet is the centerpiece of my buying strategy.**

Even if a company is expected to operate at zero earnings (breakeven) for the foreseeable future, that does not mean its stock should be trading at zero. Only the balance sheet can tell you what a fair (floor) price is in such a situation. There is simply not a situation in which you can afford to buy a common stock without assessing the balance sheet first and foremost.

Collectively, this chapter and the next illustrate the balance sheets of eight hypothetical companies. In all of the illustrations, the balance sheets are interpreted without regard to any other information about the companies. The balance sheet allows us to determine if the stockholders' equity reflects quality. In the context of stockholders' equity, I define *quality* as a balance sheet that reflects a financially healthy company through the details of its asset and liability accounts. The asset and liability detail must satisfy two quality standards: adequate liquidity and adequate solvency. If the balance sheet does not pass both of these quality standards, I ordinarily will not consider the company as a potential investment. If the standards are met, the next part of my balance-sheet assessment will be to calculate an *initial floor price* per share for the company's stock.

For the sake of simplicity, each of the eight hypothetical company balance sheets reflects stockholders' equity of $100. Further, it is assumed that each company has ten shares of common stock outstanding. Since there are ten shares outstanding, each share's equity value is $10 ($100 / 10 shares = $10). So at first glance, it may sound like an identical value is reflected on each balance sheet. However, the composition of the assets and the liabilities are the key to proper balance-sheet analysis. These examples will provide you with a feel for using the balance sheet in risk analysis and will reveal my personal approach to using the balance sheet to determine an *initial floor price* on a share of company stock.

Again, the balance sheet must pass two quality standards before I consider buying a company's stock. First, the company must reflect adequate liquidity to pay its short-term obligations. To do this, a company has to have enough liquid assets to make payroll, keep the lights on, purchase its inventory, and so forth. On the balance sheet, current assets are viewed as liquid assets. Current liabilities are viewed as a company's short-term obligations. I previously described the current ratio (current assets / current liabilities) as a common measure of balance-sheet liquidity. Under my balance-sheet analysis approach, I use a simple modification of the current ratio and call it the *adjusted current ratio* to test for adequate liquidity. My *adjusted current ratio* is calculated as follows:

Adjusted Current Ratio = (Cash + [0.80 × Noncash Current Assets]) / Current Liabilities

Using this ratio, my first test of quality is:

Quality Standard 1: Balance sheet must show an *adjusted current ratio* of 1.2 or greater.

While the current ratio is a widely accepted measure of liquidity on a balance sheet, it does not distinguish between the cash current asset and the noncash current assets (accounts receivable, inventory, etc.) in terms of the ability to settle day-to-day financial obligations. My current ratio modification, the *adjusted current ratio*, discounts the noncash current assets to 80 percent of their stated balance-sheet amounts. This discounting of noncash current assets recognizes that these assets are different than the cash asset in that they involve some uncertainty as to their true cash worth relative to settling obligations today. The ratio recognizes that cash is the most certain asset in terms of its ability to pay off current liabilities immediately, and it is, therefore, not discounted.

In summation, my *adjusted current ratio* reflects that if a company has all of its current assets in the cash form, it would take cash of just 1.2 times the stated amount of current liabilities on the balance sheet to have adequate liquidity. Again, cash is perfectly liquid, and I do not discount its stated balance-sheet amount since there is no risk concerning its true cash value. However, if a company has all of its current assets in noncash form, it would take noncash assets of 1.5 times ($1.2 / 0.8 = 1.5$) the current liabilities to have adequate liquidity. It is important to understand that my modification of the current ratio takes into account that the cash asset is more liquid than the noncash current assets in terms of its ability to pay off short-term obligations. The traditional current ratio does not recognize any difference between these assets.

If you are an experienced investor, you will be thinking of a liquidity ratio known as the quick ratio, which deducts the inventory current asset from total current assets before dividing the remaining current assets by current liabilities ([current assets – inventory] / current liabilities). This quick ratio is radically different from the current ratio in that it excludes a significant current asset on most balance sheets—namely inventory—from any consideration as a near-cash resource that can be used to pay off short-term obligations. I have not found this quick ratio to be nearly as useful as the *adjusted current ratio* I devised from years of studying balance sheets to determine when a balance sheet reflects adequate liquidity. It's not critical that you understand the derivation of my *adjusted current ratio*. Knowing how to apply it is important. We are close to the point of illustrating the use of the *adjusted current ratio*; in fact, I will illustrate its use eight times across this chapter and the next.

To address the second quality issue, recall that a balance sheet reflects the assets, liabilities, and equity of a company and that

Assets = Liabilities + Equity

and

Assets – Liabilities = Equity

The second quality requirement is that the company must have enough assets to satisfy or settle its total liabilities. That is, it must have positive equity. Clearly, if a company has more total liabilities, or obligations, than it has total assets, that company, on paper, is bankrupt (insolvent). So why would anyone buy stock in a company unless it has positive stockholders' equity? Believe me when I say people do buy companies with negative stockholders' equity all the time.

There are a host of well-known companies trading on the stock market that reflect negative stockholders' equity on their balance sheets. They stay afloat by generating enough cash to make timely interest payments on debt while carefully managing principal debt repayment through, what amounts to restructuring of debt maturities. I guess the thinking is that so long as the debt (principal) never comes due, it's not really a problem. However, that thinking is fallacious. I interpret balance sheets as though any debt will come due at some point. My practice is to invest in companies that have the financial strength reflected in their balance sheets to pay all their obligations in full and on time.

Whereas my first quality issue focuses on the adequacy of the company's liquidity to keep pace with its day-to-day operations, my second quality issue focuses on whether the company is able to satisfy its total liabilities, both short-term and long-term. Is the company clearly solvent? My second quality standard goes beyond simply making sure that total assets exceed total liabilities. Yes, if total assets exceed total liabilities, the balance sheet reflects "apparent" solvency. However, I'm not going to assume that the total assets are worth their stated balance sheet amounts in cash.

Cash is the only asset I'm willing to accept at face value. I'm going to discount all noncash assets to compensate for the risk that they might be worth less in cash than the numbers stated on the balance sheet. Noncash assets are either tangible (such as inventory, or property, plant and equipment) or intangible (such as goodwill, patents, or copyrights). Under my balance sheet approach to buying low, I discount intangible assets to zero, since assigning a cash value to something of intangible worth is virtually impossible. I simply disregard any amounts on the balance sheet for intangible asset accounts. I discount the tangible noncash assets to 90 percent of the values shown on the balance sheet. Discounting at this rate is the by-product of trial and error over many years of investing. I use a modified version of stock-holders' equity and call it *adjusted tangible stockholders' equity* to test for adequate solvency.

Assets – Liabilities = (Stockholders') Equity

and

Stockholders' Equity = Assets – Liabilities

My *adjusted tangible stockholders' equity* is calculated as follows:

Adjusted Tangible Stockholders' Equity = Cash + (0.90 × Noncash Tangible Assets) – Liabilities

Using this equation, my second test of quality is as follows:

Quality Standard 2: Balance sheet must show *adjusted tangible stockholders' equity* of zero or greater.

I use 90 percent, in my second quality standard on balance sheet solvency, versus 80 percent in my first quality standard on balance sheet liquidity because adequate liquidity is a day-to-day concern whereas adequate solvency is a longer-term concern. Companies have a bit more wiggle room to deal with overall solvency issues than with near-term liquidity issues such as paying the company's next electric bill or making payroll, for example.

If both of my quality standards are met, identifying my *initial floor price* per share is easy.

Initial Floor Price = Adjusted Tangible Stockholders' Equity / # of Common Stock Shares Outstanding

The *adjusted tangible stockholders' equity*, as the numerator of the *initial floor price* formula, is determined by the second quality standard formula on balance sheet solvency. As we work through the balance sheet illustrations, the quality issues of adequate liquidity and adequate solvency will become clear, as will how the calculations are performed. The determination of *initial floor price* will also become apparent. If the two quality standards are not met through our hypothetical balance sheets, we won't proceed further. If they are met, you will see how to calculate the *initial floor price* per share.

You may be wondering why I have two quality standards: a liquidity standard and a solvency standard. I mean, if a company is adequately solvent to have enough in tangible assets to settle its total liabilities, would it not also have adequate liquidity? That is, isn't an overall solvency standard sufficient to establish the quality of a balance sheet? It is not. A company can have ample tangible assets to settle its total liabilities and yet not have enough of those tangible assets in the form of cash or near-cash assets to make its next payroll or its next interest payment, for example. This lack of short-term liquidity can lead to technical default. My quality standards recognize that a financially sound company is one that not only has enough total asset worth to satisfy its liabilities, but also one that maintains enough of its asset base in liquid form to settle short-term obligations.

Over the years, I have deviated from adhering to my quality standards on rare occasions; it has only been when I perceive the situation a genuine exception to the rule. The circumstances would have to clearly reflect a unique situation. For example, there might be mounting evidence that a balance sheet that fails my quality standards today is likely to experience imminent positive changes, whereby the balance sheet will satisfy or exceed my standards in the foreseeable future—and the stock price is irresistibly low otherwise. I've spent a lot of time learning how to invest. Today, even when I have a real sense of a company's balance sheet being an exception to my quality standards, I keep tight boundaries on myself. I practice adherence to my quality standards in assessing company balance sheets.

We will consider four hypothetical balance sheets in this chapter and four in the next. I devised the balance sheets to illustrate how the composition of assets and liabilities affect the quality and value of the stockholders' equity.

Balance Sheet of Hypothetical Company 1:

ASSETS

Current Assets:

Cash	$100
Accounts Receivable	$0
Inventory	$0
Total Current Assets	$100

Noncurrent Assets:

Property, Plant, Equip.	$0
Goodwill	$0
TOTAL ASSETS	$100

LIABILITIES

Current Liabilities

Accounts Payable	$0
Accrued Liabilities	$0
Short-term Debt	$0
Total Current Liabilities	$0

Noncurrent Liabilities:

Long-term Debt	$0
Total Liabilities	$0

STOCKHOLDERS' EQUITY	$100
TOTAL LIAB & ST. EQUITY	$100

Company 1 reflects an extremely oversimplified balance sheet but is a good starting example. The only asset is cash, and there are no liabilities to satisfy. So the equity of $100, or $10 per share, is of the highest quality conceivable. It is perfectly liquid. That is, the equity of $100 is composed entirely of cash.

Even though a simple perusal of the balance sheet reveals that the stockholders' equity is completely made up of cash, let's look at the two quality standards I use to determine if the company's balance sheet reflects the necessary strength to make it a possible candidate for further consideration. The balance sheet cash is $100, the noncash current assets are $0, and the current liabilities are $0. So,

Adjusted Current Ratio = ($100 + [0.80 × $0]) / $0 = ($100 / $0) = ?

Even though we can't get an answer when dividing by zero, we know that the adjusted current assets are plenty adequate to settle the current liabilities as they are coming due. There are no current liabilities in this first scenario, and the company has $100 in cash. Quality standard 1 on liquidity is clearly met. Dividing by zero is impossible because the answer is infinitely high.

Let's look at the second quality standard. The cash is $100, the noncash tangible assets are $0, and the liabilities are $0. So,

Adjusted Tangible Stockholders' Equity = $100 + (0.90 × $0) – $0 = $100

The *adjusted tangible stockholders' equity* of $100 is at least $0. Thus, quality standard 2 on solvency is met. The company is clearly solvent, in that its only asset is cash of $100, and it faces no liabilities to settle whatsoever.

Since both quality standards are met on the first balance sheet, we can now calculate the *initial floor price* per share. Recall that in each balance sheet example, there are ten company shares outstanding. Since the *adjusted tangible stockholders' equity* is $100, found in testing for quality standard 2, and there are ten common stock shares outstanding,

Initial Floor Price = $100 / 10 shares = $10 per share.

Thus, at the time of this balance sheet and before blending in any other information, the $10 per share provides a risk-adjusted balance-sheet worth per share that gives you a baseline price for a share of company stock per this first balance-sheet case. This baseline price is known as the *initial floor price.*

Although many uncertainties exist with investing, there is at least one absolute: the buying process must start with proper balance-sheet analysis if your goal is to buy quality and establish *your initial floor price.*

Although many uncertainties exist with investing, there is at least one absolute: the buying process must start with proper balance-sheet analysis if your goal is to buy quality and establish your *initial floor price.*

Balance Sheet of Hypothetical Company 2:

ASSETS   LIABILITIES

Current Assets: Current Liabilities
  Cash $500   Accounts Payable $200
  Accounts Receivable $0   Accrued Liabilities $200
  Inventory $0   Short-term Debt $0
  Total Current Assets $500   Total Current Liabilities $400

Noncurrent Assets: Noncurrent Liabilities:
  Property, Plant, Equip. $0   Long-term Debt $0
  Goodwill $0   Total Liabilities $400
TOTAL ASSETS $500

                       STOCKHOLDERS' EQUITY $100
                       TOTAL LIAB. & ST. EQUITY $500

Given the balance sheet of Company 2, the company's assets are as liquid as they come: all in the form of cash. However, unlike the first balance-sheet situation, the company does have other accounts, namely current liability accounts, involved in the composition (referring to the asset and liability detail) of the company's stockholders' equity position. Remember that the stockholders' equity amount is equal to the assets less the liabilities. The stockholders' equity amount is explained by the asset and liability detail. We must therefore analyze the asset and liability detail to understand the quality and likely worth of the stockholders' equity amount as stated on the balance sheet.

With the second balance sheet, all of the company's liabilities are due within a year and include no short-term or long-term debt. Debt is a monetary liability in which money has been borrowed that must be repaid by certain future dates. Liabilities that are not considered short- or long-term debt arise when something other than money has been borrowed. These non-debt liabilities still require settlement, however, in money or services rendered. Accounts payable represents money owed to the suppliers of company inventory, for example. Accrued liabilities represent amounts owed for items such as employee salaries and utility bills.

Let's see if quality standard 1 is met; that is, does the second balance sheet reflect adequate liquidity? The cash is $500, the noncash current assets are $0, and the current liabilities are $400. So,

Adjusted Current Ratio = ($500 + [0.80 × $0]) / $400 = $500 / $400 = 1.25

The ratio is at least 1.2, so the standard is met.

To examine quality standard 2, to determine whether the company is adequately solvent, the cash is $500, the noncash tangible assets are $0, and the total liabilities are $400, so,

Adjusted Tangible Stockholders' Equity = $500 + (0.90 × $0) − $400 = $100

The amount is at least $0, so the standard is met.

Finally, since the *adjusted tangible stockholders' equity* is $100 and there are ten common stock shares outstanding,

Initial Floor Price = $100 / 10 shares = $10 a share

With this second balance sheet, the equity of $10 per share is of supreme quality, just as with the first balance-sheet case. The $400 of current liabilities can be settled from the $500 cash, leaving cash of $100. Thus, the $100 shown in stockholders' equity is of perfectly liquid composition. Simply reading the balance sheet in isolation, or without knowledge of any other financial issues relative to the company, one would assume the company could be liquidated for approximately its equity value and distributed across the ten shares for $10 a share. Thus, as with Company 1, the $10 of equity per share, based on the balance sheet, provides a substantively hard *initial floor price* for the stock.

Balance Sheet of Hypothetical Company 3:

ASSETS

Current Assets:

Cash	$400
Accounts Receivable	$50
Inventory	$50
Total Current Assets	$500

Noncurrent Assets:

Property, Plant, Equip.	$0
Goodwill	$0
TOTAL ASSETS	$500

LIABILITIES

Current Liabilities

Accounts Payable	$200
Accrued Liabilities	$200
Short-term Debt	$0
Total Current Liabilities	$400

Noncurrent Liabilities:

Long-term Debt	$0
Total Liabilities	$400

STOCKHOLDERS' EQUITY	$100
TOTAL LIAB. & ST. EQUITY	$500

With Company 3, there are assets totaling $500, and all are current, generally meaning of a liquid nature. Accounts receivable refer to amounts due from customers for goods sold to them or services rendered to them on account. Inventory represents goods yet to be sold that can be sold to generate future cash inflows. As with Company 1 and Company 2, there is no debt, and the current liability total is $400. My first quality standard recognizes that the accounts receivable current asset and the inventory current asset are noncash current assets and may not be worth their stated amounts ($50 for each) in cash value on the balance sheet. On this third balance sheet, given that cash is $400, noncash current assets are $100 ($50 of accounts receivable plus $50 of inventory), and current liabilities are $400,

Adjusted Current Ratio = ($400 + [0.80 × $100]) / $400 = $480 / $400 = 1.2

Since the ratio is at least 1.2, the first quality standard of adequate liquidity is met.

Since all noncash assets on the third balance sheet are tangible (goodwill is the only intangible asset on my hypothetical balance sheet examples, and it is $0 in this third case), we can see the following values from the balance sheet: $400 in cash, $100 in noncash tangible assets, and $400 in total liabilities.

Adjusted Tangible Stockholders' Equity = $400 + (0.90 × $100) − $400 = $90

Since the amount is at least $0, the second quality standard of adequate solvency is met.

Since the *adjusted tangible stockholders' equity* is $90 and there are 10 shares,

Initial Floor Price = $90 / 10 shares = $9 per share

The baseline balance-sheet price of $9 per share is lower than in the first two balance-sheet scenarios because a portion of the company's assets are in noncash form and were risk-adjusted to 90 percent of their stated values in recognition that those stated values may be overstated in a cash context. A portion of the accounts receivables might prove uncollectible, for example. Some customers might not pay or may pay less than is owed to the company. A portion of the inventory might not be sold, or it might be sold at a deep discount if demand is less than expected.

Discounting the noncash assets to 90 percent of their balance sheet amounts in quantifying an adjusted balance sheet worth of stockholders' equity is a conservative approach, but remember that the goal in buying stocks is to buy when the price represents minimal risk. So being conservative is essential to avoiding risk.

With this third balance sheet, there is some uncertainty relative to the first two balance-sheet cases, and uncertainty is risk. This risk is reflected in the $9 per share *initial floor price* as compared to the $10 price per share determined in both of the first two balance-sheet scenarios. The third balance sheet passes my quality standards of ample liquidity and solvency. However, the balance sheet amount of the stockholders' equity is adjusted lower for risk introduced through noncash assets on the balance sheet. So the third balance sheet reflects quality but less worth to stockholders relative to the first two situations.

Balance Sheet of Hypothetical Company 4:

ASSETS

Current Assets:

Cash	$300
Accounts Receivable	$50
Inventory	$50
Total Current Assets	$400

Noncurrent Assets:

Property, Plant, Equip.	$100
Goodwill	$0
TOTAL ASSETS	$500

LIABILITIES

Current Liabilities

Accounts Payable	$200
Accrued Liabilities	$200
Short-term Debt	$0
Total Current Liabilities	$400

Noncurrent Liabilities:

Long-term Debt	$0
Total Liabilities	$400

STOCKHOLDERS' EQUITY	$100
TOTAL LIAB. & ST. EQUITY	$500

On the Company 3 balance sheet, there are $500 in current assets and $400 in current liabilities. With Company 4, there are $400 of current assets and $100 of noncurrent assets, (property, plant, and equipment, also called "fixed assets") against $400 of current liabilities that must be satisfied in the near term. Recall that current liabilities represent obligations due within a year and therefore are generally settled from current assets, since current assets are viewed as being or becoming cash within a year's time. The noncurrent property, plant, and equipment amount of $100 in this fourth case is not viewed as liquid enough to satisfy the current liabilities.

Let's start by seeing whether the first quality standard of adequate liquidity is satisfied. Cash is $300, noncash current assets are $100 (Accounts receivable + inventory), and current liabilities are $400. So,

Adjusted Current Ratio = ($300 + [0.80 × $100]) / $400 = $380 / $400 = 0.95

The ratio is not at least 1.2, so the first quality standard is not met. The company does not reflect adequate liquidity to meet its short-term obligations according to my standard.

Since this standard is not met, in actual practice I would not go any further because this balance sheet does not satisfy my quality requirements. However, let's continue for the purpose of illustrating the point I mentioned earlier about how a company that fails to reflect adequate liquidity can yet reflect adequate solvency.

Cash is $300, noncash tangible assets are $200 (accounts receivable + inventory + property, plant, and equipment), and total liabilities are $400. Thus,

Adjusted Tangible Stockholders' Equity = $300 + (0.90 × $200) − $400 = $80

Note that the second quality standard is met because the result is at least $0. Also, note that the *adjusted tangible stockholders' equity* is $80, and therefore the *initial floor price* is $8 per share.

Initial Floor Price = $80 / 10 shares = $8 per share

However, none of this matters because the company does not meet my quality standard for adequate liquidity, and I'm not interested in buying shares in this company, regardless of the stock price. Adequate liquidity and adequate solvency are two separate quality issues, and both must be met for the balance-sheet equity number to possess the necessary quality to consider for investment. While this fourth balance sheet reflects solvency, the $8 of *adjusted tangible stockholders' equity* per share (i.e., *initial floor price*) incorporates a high potential for technical default arising from a plausible inability to pay short-term obligations. A company must not only be solvent but also liquid enough to pay bills on a timely basis.

CHAPTER 6

THE BALANCE SHEET: WHEN EQUAL IS NOT EQUAL, PART II

This chapter continues the balance-sheet illustrations. Remember, all balance sheets are not created equal.

Company 5 is different from Company 4 only in the composition of the liabilities. Instead of $400 in current liabilities, there are now $200 in current liabilities and $200 in noncurrent liabilities (long-term debt). Let's examine this balance sheet for my quality criteria. Given the $300 in cash, $100 in noncash current assets (accounts receivable + inventory), and $200 in current liabilities:

Adjusted Current Ratio = ($300 + [$100 × 0.8]) / $200 = 1.9

Since the ratio is at least 1.2, the first quality standard of adequate liquidity is met.

Balance Sheet of Hypothetical Company 5:

ASSETS

LIABILITIES

Current Assets:
Cash	$300
Accounts Receivable	$50
Inventory	$50
Total Current Assets	$400

Current Liabilities
Accounts Payable	$200
Accrued Liabilities	$0
Short-term Debt	$0
Total Current Liabilities	$200

Noncurrent Assets:
Property, Plant, Equip.	$100
Goodwill	$0
TOTAL ASSETS	$500

Noncurrent Liabilities:
Long-term Debt	$200
Total Liabilities	$400

STOCKHOLDERS' EQUITY	$100
TOTAL LIAB. & ST. EQUITY	$500

Now, let's analyze the fifth balance sheet for adequate solvency. Cash is $300, noncash tangible assets are $200 (accounts receivable + inventory + property, plant, & equipment), and total liabilities are $400. So

Adjusted Tangible Stockholders' Equity = $300 + (0.90 × $200) − $400 = $80

The second quality standard is met since the amount is at least $0.

Again, if you compare the fifth balance sheet to the fourth, you will note that the only difference is with the liability composition. The amount of liabilities is $400 in both cases, but $200 of the liabilities that had to be settled within a year in case 4 do not have to be settled in that time frame in case 5. That is, $200 of the $400 in case 5 is in noncurrent liability form, meaning that it will not come due within the next twelve months. The company has more time to come up with the cash to settle this $200, and this is reflected in an adequate liquidity rating for Company 5, whereas the adequate liquidity standard was not met with Company 4. Given the *adjusted tangible stockholders' equity* of $80,

Initial Floor Price = $80 / 10 shares = $8 per share

Company 5, by its balance-sheet detail of assets and liabilities, reveals a baseline value of $8 per common share.

Balance Sheet of Hypothetical Company 6:

ASSETS

Current Assets:
Cash	$300
Accounts Receivable	$50
Inventory	$50
Total Current Assets	$400

Noncurrent Assets:
Property, Plant, Equip.	$50
Goodwill	$50
TOTAL ASSETS	$500

LIABILITIES

Current Liabilities
Accounts Payable	$200
Accrued Liabilities	$0
Short-term Debt	$0
Total Current Liabilities	$200

Noncurrent Liabilities:
Long-term Debt	$200
Total Liabilities	$400

STOCKHOLDERS' EQUITY	$100
TOTAL LIAB. & ST. EQUITY	$500

The sixth case introduces the presence of an intangible asset on the balance sheet, namely the goodwill asset. Instead of $100 in the property, plant, and equipment account, as with Company 5, there is now $50 in that account and $50 in the goodwill account. There are no other changes. Goodwill is an intangible asset that arises from a company having purchased another company. So the company we are considering here has previously purchased one or more other companies.

Goodwill represents an intangible that is extremely difficult to value. It represents an amount paid above the fair value of specific net assets acquired and is paid, theoretically speaking, for the above average earnings that should result from the acquisition. A company will surely face difficulty going to a bank or other lender in hopes of using goodwill as collateral for a loan. As I wrote earlier, my practice when assessing the balance sheet to determine its quality in route to determining an *initial floor price* is to treat intangible assets as having a $0 value. Given the $300 of cash, noncash current assets of $100, and current liabilities of $200 with Company 6:

Adjusted Current Ratio = ($300 + [0.80 × $100]) / $200 = 1.9

My first quality standard of adequate liquidity is met, because the ratio is at least 1.2.

Moving to the assessment of adequate solvency, the cash is $300, noncash tangible assets are equal to $150 (accounts receivable + inventory + property, plant, and equipment), and total liabilities are $400:

Adjusted Tangible Stockholders' Equity = $300 + (0.90 × $150) − $400 = $35

Note that my quality standard formula for determining the *adjusted tangible stockholders' equity* automatically excludes the $50 of goodwill. That is, the formula conservatively takes into account only the tangible assets on the balance sheet (the cash amount and 90 percent of the noncash tangible assets). Given the $35 of *adjusted tangible stockholders' equity* and ten shares of stock,

Initial Floor Price = $35 / 10 shares = $3.50 per share.

It is significant to note the impact to the baseline value per share with the introduction of goodwill to the balance sheet.

Balance Sheet of Hypothetical Company 7:

ASSETS

LIABILITIES

Current Assets:

Cash	$400
Accounts Receivable	$0
Inventory	$0
Total Current Assets	$400

Current Liabilities

Accounts Payable	$200
Accrued Liabilities	$0
Short-term Debt	$0
Total Current Liabilities	$200

Noncurrent Assets:

Property, Plant, Equip.	$0
Goodwill	$100
TOTAL ASSETS	$500

Noncurrent Liabilities:

Long-term Debt	$200
Total Liabilities	$400

STOCKHOLDERS' EQUITY	$100
TOTAL LIAB. & ST. EQUITY	$500

With Company 7, all current assets are in the form of cash. The only noncurrent asset is goodwill of $100. Given the cash of $400, no noncash current assets, and $200 of current liabilities:

Adjusted Current Ratio = ($400 + [0.80 × $0]) / $200 = 2

Since the quality standard for adequate liquidity is a ratio of at least 1.2, Company 7 clearly meets the standard.

Given the cash of $400, noncash tangible assets of $0, and total liabilities of $400:

Adjusted Tangible Stockholders' Equity = $400 + (0.90 × $0) − $400 = $0

The second standard of quality requires that the *adjusted tangible stockholders' equity* be $0 or greater. The second standard's threshold is met without any to spare. Given the $0 amount and 10 shares,

Initial Floor Price = $0 / 10 shares = $0 per share

The seventh company is able to settle its short-term obligations given its *adjusted current ratio* and is therefore liquid enough to sustain operations in the near term. However, the company is on the brink of being insolvent, given its *adjusted tangible stockholders' equity* of $0. Chapter 7 will explain the necessity of blending future performance (earnings) expectations with the *initial floor price* derived from balance sheet analysis to determine an *adjusted floor price* on a share of stock. I want to buy a quality stock at, or below, its *adjusted floor price*. Even though the *initial floor price* per share on Company 7 is $0, the *adjusted floor price* could be above $0 if the company has some basis of assuming positive future earnings per share (i.e., profitability).

Balance Sheet of Hypothetical Company 8:

ASSETS

LIABILITIES

Current Assets:

Cash	$300
Accounts Receivable	$0
Inventory	$0
Total Current Assets	$300

Current Liabilities

Accounts Payable	$200
Accrued Liabilities	$0
Short-term Debt	$0
Total Current Liabilities	$200

Noncurrent Assets:

Property, Plant, Equip.	$0
Goodwill	$200
TOTAL ASSETS	$500

Noncurrent Liabilities:

Long-term Debt	$200
Total Liabilities	$400

STOCKHOLDERS' EQUITY	$100
TOTAL LIAB. & ST. EQUITY	$500

On balance sheet 8, there is $300 cash, no noncash current assets, and $200 of current liabilities. So,

Adjusted Current Ratio = ($300 + [0.80 × $0]) / $200 = 1.5

The first quality standard of adequate liquidity is achieved because the ratio exceeds the required minimum of 1.2.

Given the $300 cash amount, $0 in noncash tangible assets, and $400 in total liabilities,

Adjusted Tangible Stockholders' Equity = $300 + (0.90 × $0) − $400 = −$100

The second quality standard of adequate solvency is not met; the negative amount of $100 falls short of the required minimum of $0. There is no need to determine the *initial floor price* in this case since the second quality standard is not met.

If you recall Company 4, the adequate liquidity standard was not met even though the adequate solvency standard was satisfied. With Company 8, the adequate liquidity standard is achieved, but the adequate solvency standard is not met. Under my balance-sheet buying strategy, both quality standards must be met.

In my eight hypothetical balance sheet examples, there are no intangible assets other than goodwill. However, keep in mind that a company could have intangible assets (patents, copyrights, and so forth) other than goodwill, and, following my balance-sheet approach to finding an *initial floor price* per share, you would need to disregard them in the determination of the *adjusted tangible stockholders' equity*. So, all intangible asset balance-sheet amounts are excluded from the determination of an *initial floor price* per share under my balance-sheet assessment approach.

On the balance sheets of real companies that have both goodwill and other intangibles, you will find in the noncurrent asset section a line item called "goodwill" and another line item called "intangible assets"—the latter line item capturing the sum of all intangibles other than goodwill. Total intangible assets would be the sum of the goodwill line amount and the intangible assets line amount.

Keep in mind that buying a share of a company is buying a unit of its equity. When buying a share of common stock, you are buying a share of stockholders' equity. Stockholders' equity is a number on the balance sheet that reflects the balance sheet's worth. That is, the stockholders' equity amount reflects the balance-sheet representation of what company stockholders are worth at a point in time. The stockholders' equity amount shown on the balance sheet is also referred to as "net worth," "net assets," or "book value."

I hope you are starting to see what I'm doing in deriving an *initial floor price* per share from the balance sheet. I'm simply recognizing that when I buy a stock, I'm buying a unit of the company's stockholders' equity as reflected on its balance sheet. My approach is to ensure that I don't pay more for that ownership stake than it's conservatively worth at the time of my buying.

The worth of the company stockholders' equity, as stated on the balance sheet, should be called into question if there is evidence that the equity amount lacks quality—namely inadequate liquidity or solvency. That can only be determined by looking at the asset and liability composition of the stockholders' equity, just as we have been doing with these hypothetical balance-sheet scenarios. If the stockholders' equity lacks quality, the stock should be avoided.

The stated stockholders' equity worth on each of the eight balance sheets presented is $100. In each case, there are ten shares of stock. So without analyzing the assets and liabilities, it first appears that each balance sheet has a worth per share of $10 ($100 / 10 shares = $10). However, a balance sheet that is less liquid in its asset composition, is inclusive of assets that are intangible in nature, and is saddled with significant current liabilities is one that is of increasingly questionable quality. Therefore, the stockholders' equity amount should pass the quality tests of adequate liquidity and adequate solvency before you consider purchasing the stock.

Even if those tests of quality are passed, the equity must be adjusted downward for any identified weakness in balance-sheet quality. After assuring that quality standards of liquidity and solvency are met, my *adjusted tangible stockholders' equity* calculated amount can be used in ascertaining an *initial floor price* per share. The *adjusted tangible stockholders' equity* calculation incorporates the downward adjustments for noncash tangible assets (limits inclusion of these less liquid assets to 0.90 of their stated balance-sheet amounts) and for intangible assets (excludes balance-sheet amounts on these highly illiquid assets).

The eight balance sheet scenarios clearly express the meaning of my introductory statements in the last two chapters: *all balance sheets are not created equal.* Companies with equal balance-sheet stockholders' equity per share may have different *initial floor (stock) prices* based on the composition of the assets and liabilities.

The point of this book is to show the essentiality of the balance sheet when it comes to identifying low prices on the common stock of solid companies. Without the balance sheet, it is impossible to determine whether the company reflects the financial health, or flexibility, to take advantage of opportunities that may exist. The balance sheet reflects a value that is already booked and, through its asset and liability detail, the quality of that value.

There are too many factors in the universe of possibilities to include every one into your stock valuation analysis. However, the balance sheet is a static report. It incorporates into asset and liability account balances the entire company history of all recorded financial events from the company beginning to date. The latest balance sheet, without doubt, is the best resource for assessing an *initial floor price* for a share of common stock. The balance sheet does not include any forecasted numbers. Rather, it summarizes the impact of all past financial events into a set of account balances that reflect the present financial condition; therefore, it does not assume anything yet to come. It reflects a current standing of financial worth referred to as stockholders' equity and the quality of that equity in both asset and liability account balances.

The balance sheet is not a what-if report. It is a what-is report. It is the most objective basis available to get at an *initial floor stock price*. Remember there are enough stocks out there that you can always buy low. You must choose to be disciplined and never swayed by any momentary hype surrounding a stock in your buying behavior. You might find success occasionally by following the crowd, but you will likely miss out on the truly big returns and, conversely, suffer losses, perhaps substantial ones.

I've used the expression *initial floor price* to refer to a value per share derived from the balance-sheet analysis. The word *initial* suggests that there is more to do before finding a buying price on a good stock. The outlook for earnings is important in terms of assessing the likely return on your investment dollar, and this book does not diminish the importance of the earnings outlook. However, determining how many dollars you are willing to invest in a share of a company cannot be assessed by looking only at the possible return on the dollar invested.

Earnings are inherently risky (uncertain) unless completely locked in by contracts. However, a solid *adjusted tangible stockholders' equity* per share (*initial floor price*) close to the current stock price on the market makes an attractive earnings outlook all the more attractive. The preservation of the invested dollar, then, is not as highly dependent on the earnings outlook becoming reality. In other words, if you buy a share close to what is determined to be a solid equity per share (*initial floor price*) based on proper balance-sheet assessment, you have put yourself in a position to gain big if a good earnings outlook becomes reality, or, conversely, in a position to avoid losing a significant amount of your investment if good earnings fail to materialize.

These chapters provided a series of hypothetical balance sheets to illustrate how the balance sheet can reveal the quality of existing equity, such that an *initial floor price* for a stock can be gauged aside from the outlook for earnings. Again, assessing the existing equity provides a means of turning risk aversion into practical minimizing of risk when it comes to buying common stocks. Additionally, it provides a context for properly assessing the value of projected earnings.

Buying low is not optional, but essential to consistently making money in the stock market. Buying low is not simply buying at a price lower than that at which you sell. Selling a stock for more than its cost does not automatically mean that the stock was purchased at a low price. The only relevant context for defining a low stock price is proper analysis of the balance sheet's stockholders' equity!

> **Buying low is not optional, but essential to consistently making money in the stock market.**

CHAPTER 7

BLENDING MARKET EXPECTATIONS WITH BALANCE-SHEET ASSESSMENT

If past history was all there was to the game, the richest people would be librarians.[2]
—Warren Buffett

Making the balance sheet the foundational basis for buying stocks is a commonsense approach. As an accounting professor for many years, I've observed that a balance-sheet focus in buying stocks is not practiced due to the widespread idea that the balance sheet is not readable unless you are an accountant. However, that is simply not true. Accountants provide the information. An investor needs to know how to use the information, not how to provide it.

In some cases, an extensive accounting background might cause a person to become so entrenched in following the rules to provide the information that he or she is unable to step back and properly interpret the end product as a potential investor.

---

[2] See Warren Buffett under Popular Authors at www.brainyquote.com

To use the balance sheet for analyzing common stocks, you simply must be willing to expend the effort to understand the nature of the accounts found on the balance sheet with regard to what they communicate concerning the following:

(1) The quality of the stockholders' equity

(2) A conservative cash value of stockholders' equity

Let's review some balance-sheet basics. The corporate balance sheet shows a company's stockholders' equity and also the assets and liabilities that detail the equity. Assets enlarge equity, whereas liabilities diminish equity. So equity is measured as the excess of assets above liabilities. Equity on the balance sheet represents the amount belonging to stockholders at a specific date and is valued according to a set of accounting rules.

Three major (accounting) financial statements are produced: one that represents the present financial position (balance sheet); one that reflects the recent operating performance (income statement); and one that reflects the recent cash-flow activity (statement of cash flows) of the company. The accounting value, known as book value, net asset value, or net worth, is *only* reflected on the balance sheet and is referred to there as stockholders' equity. The balance sheet is the single statement that shows where the company stands today financially. It is therefore the focal point of my analysis when it comes to buying quality stocks at low prices.

The amount of the stockholders' equity shown on the balance sheet would rarely be a perfectly accurate representation of what the shareholder equity is actually worth according to the stock market's pricing of a share of equity (stock) around that balance-sheet date. Remember, a share of common stock represents a share of the company's equity, and equity is found on the balance sheet, as stockholders' equity. So why isn't a share of equity always priced on the market to equal the balance-sheet equity (stockholders' equity) per share? There are three major reasons.

First, consider the prior two chapters. The hypothetical balance sheets of those chapters reveal that all balance-sheet equity balances are not created equal. Different companies can have an equal amount of stockholders' equity and an equal number of stock shares for that stockholders' equity to be spread over, yet the quality of the stockholders' equity can vary widely across the companies, given the asset and liability composition of that stockholders' equity. Thus, it is absolutely logical that the stock market should legitimately appraise companies differently based on the asset and liability composition of the stockholders' equity. That is, the stock price on the market can differ from the accounting value of the stockholders' equity on the balance sheet based on the quality of that equity.

A second reason for the stock price on the market differing from the accounting (stockholders' equity) worth per share is that accounting does not update all of the asset and liability accounts to their appraised values at each balance-sheet date; some accounting numbers are not going to perfectly represent true market values. Certainly, cash and near-cash assets will come closer to reflecting true market values than will noncurrent assets, the latter being inclusive of not only tangible assets including buildings and machinery, for example, but also the most difficult assets to value, namely intangibles. The noncurrent assets are generally carried on the balance sheet, from one accounting period to the next, using their original cost (i.e., purchase price) as the basis for valuation under generally accepted accounting rules. Thus, their accounting values can become out of sync with their market values as time passes.

A third reason behind the difference between the accounting value of an equity share and the current stock price is that the balance sheet is a summation of all accounting events having occurred to date. It does not include forecasted events that the market will attempt to factor in when assigning a fair price on the stock. My buying approach recognizes that future earnings should be factored into the buying decision. We are not quite ready for the detailed explanation of calculating the *adjusted floor price,* but the adjustment of my *initial floor price* is explained by how I factor in future company earnings. That is, the difference in *adjusted floor price* and *initial floor price* is the consideration I give to the forecasted earnings of the company.

In my experience, the market does not merely factor in forecasted earnings to the buying decision. The market is, in fact, preoccupied with forecasted earnings—to the virtual exclusion of the balance sheet as a consideration relative to buying common stocks. Certainly, the market does not use the balance sheet as the primary consideration in determining low buying prices on common stocks. I'll stick with my approach. It is why my returns have outpaced market returns by a wide margin.

So the stockholders' equity amount on today's balance sheet is not likely to be precisely representative of the current company worth on the market as reflected by the stock price because of the following considerations:

1) Stockholders' equity varies in its quality, depending on the composition of the assets and liabilities which comprise it.

2) Stockholders' equity is comprised of net assets (assets less liabilities), which are valued based on accounting rules. In large measure, the rules do not require that asset values be updated at each balance-sheet date to reflect the most recent fair market values.

3) Stockholders' equity does not incorporate any future expected performance (earnings) that will change the amount and composition (asset and liability detail) of the stockholders' equity on future balance sheets.

Through my approach for determining an *initial floor price* per share, I am addressing the first two reasons for variation in the market's pricing and the amount of stockholders' equity on the balance sheet. By adjusting my *initial floor price* to an *adjusted floor price* to account for the effect of anticipated future earnings, my buying approach addresses the third reason for variation in market pricing.

After finding the *initial floor price,* I next consider the impact of future performance expectations over the next twelve months on my *initial floor price.* Future earnings will change the balance-sheet stockholders' equity amount and its asset and liability composition. If my evaluation of stockholders' equity today leads me to an *initial floor price* for the company stock of $10 per share, and earnings next year are forecasted to be $1 per share, then holding all other things constant, my initial number of $10 per share will improve to $11 a share over the next year, should the $1 earnings per share forecast come true. That is, the balance-sheet stockholders' equity per share will grow by the amount of earnings per share, since company earnings become a part of the balance sheet.

Under my buying approach, I will add the $1 of forecasted earnings per share (EPS) for the next twelve months to my $10 balance-sheet assessment number, the *initial floor price,* which gives me an *adjusted floor price* of $11 per share. At $11 per share or less, I am interested in buying the stock. My long-term use of the balance-sheet buying strategy has been so honed that I've found that adding the next twelve months of expected (forecasted) EPS to the *initial floor price* to find my *adjusted floor price* is a dependable approach to minimizing risk to a low level while leaving me with a pool of stocks to pick from that meet my stringent buying criteria.

Much can happen in a year's time, so there is risk involved in adding a year's worth of forecasted EPS to my *initial floor price* to derive my *adjusted floor price.* However, companies can predict the short term with more certainty than the long term. I'm defining *short term* here as the next twelve months. So adding expected performance predicted beyond the next twelve months involves a level of performance certainty I am unwilling to assume when I buy a stock.

With many small companies, there is a lack of financial analyst coverage that would provide projections on future earnings. My practice is to substitute the past twelve months' earnings per share (EPS) for the future twelve months' EPS forecast when estimates of future earnings are not available. The past twelve months of EPS will be available on any company since the earnings are known. The past twelve months' EPS is referred to as trailing-twelve-month, or TTM, EPS. This TTM nomenclature is applied to other financial metrics too, not just to earnings. One example would be TTM sales, which means company sales over the past twelve months.

Simply stated, my approach blends market expectations with balance-sheet assessment by adding expected EPS for the next twelve months to the *initial floor price* per share to derive an *adjusted floor price* per share. At this *adjusted floor price* or below, I'm willing to consider buying.

Adjusted Floor Price = Initial Floor Price + Expected Twelve-Month EPS

Again, accounting rules do not have to be understood for the balance sheet to serve its purpose of enabling the investment community to see a representation of where the company stands financially at a given time. In addition to knowing a balance sheet's three elements, namely assets, liabilities, and equities, a basic understanding of the nature of assets (tangible vs. intangible) is important. The timing of required liability settlements (current vs. noncurrent) must also be observed.

Buying common stocks without evaluation of the balance sheet creates a significant risk that would otherwise not exist. That's because it is impossible to determine whether I'm paying too much without having reviewed the company's stockholders' equity found on the balance sheet. The balance sheet exists, in large part, to allow for the mitigation of the risk of buying a stock at too high a price.

> The balance sheet exists, in large part, to allow for the mitigation of the risk of buying a stock at too high a price.

A company cannot take advantage of opportunities it may have without solid balance-sheet support. A weak balance sheet will stifle opportunity, unless the company can sell its story to new financiers who are willing to speculate on a company's future growth and, accordingly, strengthen the company's equity position with an infusion of investment capital, or new money.

I cannot overstate the significance of assessing the balance-sheet worth properly before buying a stock. If you have some prior investment experience, you know that the observation of earnings is often the only factor considered when it comes to stock valuation. A significant number of companies today are trading at lofty prices, some for hundreds of dollars per share because earnings are growing quickly, yet their stockholders' equity per share from the balance sheet is barely above zero—and sometimes even negative, meaning that the balance sheet reflects insolvency. If intangibles are excluded, the tangible stockholders' equity per share is actually extremely negative in many of these companies.

The companies keep going because they are maintaining sufficient cash inflows to stay liquid enough to pay current obligations. If earnings slow or turn negative, the balance sheet will come into play, and stock prices will plummet. I've learned from past mistakes that I'm not interested in this kind of investment. I'll let someone else buy the big earnings and growth story when the company lacks balance-sheet support for the existing stock price.

There is no contradiction between the concepts that the balance sheet is the foundational basis for buying solid companies at low prices and that stock prices are driven by a company's future performance, as measured by earnings. Future earnings will be added to the balance-sheet stockholders' equity as the earnings actually transpire and thus make the company worth more. However, it is the very uncertainty of future earnings that makes buying a stock strictly based on them a very bad approach to buying common stocks. Future earnings cannot tell you where the floor stock price for a company may be. The balance sheet cannot perfectly tell you where it is; accounting rules are imperfect, and the balance sheet does not incorporate any future expectations. That said, analysis of the balance sheet will get you a lot closer to the floor stock price in a worst-case scenario where future earnings fail to meet expectations and lead to a sell-off of the stock.

So this is where we've come. Balance sheet assessment is the foundation for determining an *initial floor price* per share, which excludes any future performance assumptions. Then evaluation of a company's future earnings prospects can be used to adjust the *initial floor price*. If a company is expected to lose money over the next twelve months, the balance sheet *initial floor price* may be too high, since the losses will eat away at existing balance-sheet stockholders' equity. For example, if the *initial floor price* is $10 per share and the company is expected to lose $2 a share the coming year, ideally, you do not want to pay more than $8 a share. Remember to blend expected EPS for the next twelve months with the *initial floor price* per share to find the buying price: the *adjusted floor price* per share:

Adjusted Floor Price = *Initial Floor Price* + Expected Twelve-Month EPS

In my example here:

Adjusted Floor Price = $10 + (–$2) = $8 per share

Actually, you would prefer to pay considerably less than $8 per share unless the company can clearly reveal a path to profitability, say, in the next two years. A company that is not profitable may be trading cheaply enough to flash a buy signal according to my *adjusted floor price* per share criterion. However, losses reduce stockholders' equity and therefore work against an equity investment. My practice is to stick with companies that have a track record of profitability.

By now, you can tell how risk averse I am, and I'm sure you are too. I mean, who wants to lose money? Yes, investing in stocks involves taking risk. Remember, risk is the downside, while reward is the upside. Additionally, it is a financial truth in investing that risk drives return. That is, to realize return, I must be willing to assume risk. However, my approach is to greatly minimize my risk by selecting the best quality at the cheapest price. By doing so, I increase the probability of realizing those sought-after high returns. My approach recognizes that I must know how to determine a conservative value of equity before I take a financial stake in that equity. Without the balance sheet, determining the conservative value of equity is simply impossible.

Permit me to expound a bit further on the notion of risk. *Uncertainty* is a synonym for risk. Risk with stocks involves the degree of uncertainty surrounding a company's future expected operating performance. The more uncertain the future expected profits for a company, the wider is the potential variation between expected profits and the actual profits. So when the risk associated with future profits is high, the profits (return) could be much lower than expected or much higher than expected. Your objective is to avoid buying when the potential for realizing a return lower than what is expected is still present in the current stock price. You want to buy when the worst concerns have "already" been factored into the stock price. By doing so, you avoid taking anything but minimal risk of loss to your invested capital.

> **You want to buy when the worst concerns have "already" been factored into the stock price.**

You may yet witness a bit more price decline after you buy, but your situation becomes one of having the objective prospect of likely realizing a good return, and potentially a significant return if better-than-expected earnings occur at some point in the future. The key to locating quality stocks trading at low prices is using the balance sheet to determine the *initial floor price* per share and then making a conservative adjustment to that price for expected EPS over the coming twelve months to get the *adjusted floor price* per share (i.e., the target price to consider the stock a buy—at this price or below).

This book is focused on buying stocks low, not on selling stocks high. However, remember this concept. You are buying low when the uncertainty of expected earnings is reflected in the stock price. You are selling high when the certainty of expected earnings is reflected in the stock price.

Since the focus in this book is on buying low, it is reasonable that if a stock price reflects the uncertainty of future earnings, it is probably not priced significantly above its assessed stockholders' equity worth (*initial floor price*). That is, if the market has decided that future earnings are without any real degree of certainty, the stock price is probably searching for a floor level. This floor level would logically be tied to the probable worth of the stockholders' equity (the *adjusted tangible stockholders' equity*), as detailed by the balance sheet.

You want to buy when folks are feeling uncertain about the future, not when they are feeling confident. A healthy balance sheet underlying an unhealthy stock price often implies an opportunity. After buying into a situation like this, eventual clarity on future earnings will typically act as a release on the compressed stock price. This is often true even if clarity comes in the form of concerns over future earnings being validated by actual results that are below expectations.

> A healthy balance sheet underlying an unhealthy stock price often implies an opportunity.

Without proper balance-sheet assessment, one is left to "feel" a certain way about future earnings in deciding when to buy. You can read a stock price chart to see how folks are "feeling" about a company's future at any given moment. Stock charts show the trending patterns of a stock price on the market. Don't misunderstand me. My desire is not to dismiss stock charts or any available information that can contribute to the investment process. However, I am trying to boldly posit that you must have the right foundation for investing in common stocks if you want to take an objective position on what a low stock price looks like. If you are buying low consistently, don't expect the crowd to be moving in the same direction with you. There is no place in the stock market for emotional investing, not unless you are willing to lose a lot of money. Rely on the balance sheet to make the decision for you.

This approach will work in buying common stock in companies of any size. However, most often, stocks that meet my stringent buying criteria are small companies that are flying below the radar. Large companies will not generally be priced low enough to hit my *adjusted floor price* unless the market is experiencing a major downward correction during which fear is prevalent in most stock prices. In early 2009, when the Dow Jones Index fell well below 7,000, a substantial number of large companies reached prices low enough to meet my buying standards.

If you make sure your stock purchases pass balance-sheet scrutiny—meaning that you decline to buy stocks that are interesting but don't meet your low-price criteria—you will undoubtedly occasionally miss out on stocks with which you would have done well had you purchased them. However, you will cut investment losses greatly by avoiding most of the situations that would have eroded your invested dollars. Additionally, the stocks you do buy will stand a real chance of making solid returns.

Some folks say today that "buy and hold" is an outdated investment practice. While you probably should not keep holding if a stock becomes fully valued or if its future becomes increasingly less optimistic, that does not mean buy and hold is no longer practical. Some companies you invest in may do really well, and this will be reflected in the stock price reaching your target to sell, thereby justifying selling the stock and repositioning the funds into another quality company selling at a low stock price. Other companies you invest in may come upon hard times or start to reveal evidence of mismanagement, thereby justifying selling the stock to cut your losses and transitioning the funds to a better opportunity. After all, "hold" does not literally mean holding forever.

In my view, the useful meaning of "buy and hold" is to buy quality at a low price and hold it until its true value becomes recognized by the market. This true value could result in gains or losses. However, my methodology for finding quality stocks trading at low prices lessens the risk of incurring substantive losses and increases the probability of realizing substantive gains. If you are fortunate enough to buy a quality company stock at a low price early in a prolonged growth period, your holding period may be for years.

> In my view, the useful meaning of "buy and hold" is to buy quality at a low price and hold it until its true value becomes recognized by the market.

Of course, mature companies that are steady performers and that provide a regular dividend payout offer the best opportunities for holding a position in perpetuity. However, while the idea of buying low applies in that these established companies should only be selected when they are down in price relative to value, the significant returns possible from common stock investments do not generally reside in the companies that have grown into mature behemoths. They have already arrived. The big returns can be realized on companies that have a lot of room for growth. In the next chapter, I will discuss how investing in small companies sporting great balance sheets and solid track records of profitability may offer the best opportunities to buy at incredibly low prices.

CHAPTER 8

IDENTIFYING SMALL-COMPANY STOCKS AT GREAT BUY-IN PRICES

It is noteworthy to point out a significant factor that has contributed to the success of my annualized returns. That factor is my tendency to buy smaller (market) capitalization stocks of solid companies. Market capitalization is calculated as the company's current stock price per share multiplied by the number of company common stock shares outstanding. So if a company has 2 million shares outstanding and its shares currently trade at $10 a share, the company's market capitalization is $20 million (2M shares × $10 price per share = $20M). I will use the words *market cap* to refer to market capitalization going forward.

When professional stock analysts (i.e., Credit Suisse, Citigroup, UBS, etc.) cover a stock, they generally offer a buy, hold, or sell opinion on the stock. To support their opinion, they offer estimates of future EPS and generally give a target stock price that they believe will be realized within the next twelve months. A large-cap company usually has wide attention from the investment community and therefore has a number of analysts that cover its stock. Investors often buy shares in these big companies simply based on the analysts' opinions. An investor can make money in the stock market this way, but the returns are not likely to be more significant than broad market average returns, since all investors have ready access to the analyst opinions.

With the small-company (small-cap) stocks, many are well-established, profitable entities that lack current analyst coverage. This lack of analyst coverage can signal that the investment community is not broadly aware of the company, and thus it is possible for an investor who knows how to assess a company's value to buy shares at bargain prices before some event draws attention to the company's deep value, sending the stock price markedly higher. Among the world of stocks, stocks of small but solid businesses for which analyst coverage is often lacking can provide the largest return potential. My largest stock returns have been realized as a result of applying my balance-sheet buying strategy toward small-cap stocks.

Again large-cap companies are already closely followed by the investment community. These companies are not waiting to be discovered. Therefore the stocks of big companies rarely see their prices get as low, relative to the likely worth of the stockholders' equity, as do small company stocks. My strategy is practical in finding low prices on quality stocks of companies of all sizes. I find the most outstanding buys, though, in the small-cap arena. With small-cap stocks, I'm playing the role of stock analyst in the absence of analyst coverage, and it is in this segment of the stock market that the potential rewards of my strategy are most pronounced.

Many today erroneously conclude that a small company is automatically much riskier than a large company and therefore is overpriced on a relative basis. That is, many would say it is always safer to buy the large company, without exception. However, the balance sheet is the balancing (pun intended) factor. It tells a story that can reveal a risky and pricey large company versus a safe and inexpensive small company. Although there are several risks factors associated with small companies that are not as common to large companies, the absence of analyst coverage among many of the small companies can actually reflect an opportunity. Because I'm comfortable using the balance sheet to ascertain an *initial floor price*, it is easy to identify gem companies trading at bargain prices.

It is not uncommon for a small company to be so far off investor radar screens as to have settled at a price well below any semblance of reasonableness. Due to being overlooked from a lack attention, the stock can trade well below its *adjusted floor price* (the *initial floor price* adjusted for EPS over the next twelve months). The key to identifying these value-laden little gems is, of course, proper analysis of the balance sheet.

Market inefficiencies are far more commonplace in the world of small-cap stocks also because they often lack attention from institutional investors, including mutual funds, to hold positions in the stocks. So while large, well-followed companies do not typically get extremely mispriced to the downside, this mispricing is not that uncommon among the smaller companies. A large-company stock will rarely see its current price multiplied once over within a year or two, much less in a period of several months. However, witnessing a stock price multiply several times in a short period of time is not that strange in the world of small company stocks, especially those identified as micro caps. A micro-cap company is one that generally has a market capitalization of between $50 million and $300 million.

> A large-company stock will rarely see its current price multiplied once over within a year or two, much less in a period of several months. However, witnessing a stock price multiply several times in a short period of time is not that strange in the world of small company stocks, especially those identified as micro caps.

When I was just a small boy, time seemed to pass slowly, but now it seems to fly. A year seemed forever back then, but today a year is a small ripple on a large lake. An explanation was offered to me once. It goes like this. When a child goes from one to two years of age, the second year is 100 percent of the child's former life ([2–1] / 1 = 1, or 100%). When a person goes from fifty years of age to fifty-one, the fifty-first year is but 2 percent of his or her former life ([51 – 50] / 50 = 0.02, or 2%). Thus, as a person's life increases in years lived, each next year becomes less than what it was before as a percentage of one's overall life. Yet a year is a year. In terms of absolute years, going from one to two years is the same as going from fifty to fifty-one years. Nonetheless, the next year does not represent as much time as it did before on a relative (percentage) basis as life progresses.

Permit me to transfer this explanation into the arena of stock investing. Small company stocks will trade in the single digits far more often that their larger peers. It is easier to grow fast from a small base number than it is from a large base number. Now a dollar is a dollar. Nonetheless, a stock that costs $1 today and is sold for $2 in six months produces a 100 percent return over that period. A stock that costs $50 today and is sold for $51 in six months produces a 2 percent return over an equal period. In absolute terms, both stocks increased by $1. On a relative basis, the stock costing $1 outperformed the stock costing $50 to the tune of fifty times (100% / 2% = 50).

Let me interject here that when I refer to small companies that have a low price, I am not referring to what is generally known in the stock market as penny stocks. Yes, stocks regarded as penny stocks are often defined as those that have a low price and low market cap, but there is more. True penny stocks frequently trade on the over-the-counter bulletin board (OTCBB) or through another trading platform known as the Pink Sheets. Neither of these trading platforms represents a major stock exchange. Examples of major well-known US stock exchanges are NASDAQ Stock Market and the New York Stock Exchange (NYSE).

Some define a penny stock so broadly as to include any stock that trades below $5 a share. However, many of the large-cap companies including Ford Motor Company (F), for example, traded below $5 a share during the recession that ravaged stock prices in the latter part of 2008 and into 2009. Ford actually traded down to near $1 during November 2008. However, Ford clearly is not a penny stock in any sense of what is meant by penny stock.

My personal version of a true penny stock is one I define as including *all* of the following attributes: not well regulated, does not trade over a major open stock exchange, reflects distressed financials (especially balance sheet), has no history of substantive revenue production or of profitability, and is very speculative in terms of when, and if, it might ever become profitable. You may have received e-mails, text messages, or faxes advertising these stocks with enticing words about how you can make a quick fortune if you buy them *now*. Including this kind of stock in the field of potential investments violates everything I have written in this book. I don't buy what I consider to be true penny stocks and do not advocate buying them since I believe they carry excessive risks that are too difficult to measure.

I will buy a stock that might be trading below a dollar, but only when the balance sheet reflects a financially sound business and the company has been conducting operations for a good number of years, having experienced profitability previously and with the prospect of improved profitability over coming years. While such stock purchases are irregular compared to the buying of other stocks, these low-priced stocks I've bought here and there over the years don't represent stocks that fall under my personal definition of true penny stocks. I only buy when my risk is minimal relative to the gains I could experience. I'm not going to invest in a company that lacks a sufficient history to analyze. The balance sheet is always central for me in deciding what and when to buy.

I have bought several micro caps over the years that were obviously extremely mispriced on the low side based on the balance sheet. That is, I bought at or below my calculated *adjusted floor price* per share. I mentioned before that most investors buy stocks based on earnings without much regard for the balance sheet. The fact is that professional stock analysts who cover the well-known stocks form their buy, hold, and sell opinions based on projections of earnings amounts and earnings growth rates;

growth rates are usually projected five years out. It only takes reading one analyst's report to see that an analyst's opinion is formed primarily on forecasted earnings with little attention to the balance sheet.

With micro-cap companies, buying low would often not be definable by expected future earnings since there are usually no financial analysts covering the companies and therefore no available earnings expectations. Buying low, then, must be defined without access to profit forecasts. The lack of analyst projections on earnings probably explains, in large measure, why many investors shy away from looking at small-cap companies as a serious investment option. Avoidance of the stocks leaves a dearth of demand, permitting the stocks to sometimes trade well below the *adjusted floor price* per share. You simply have to know how to assess the balance sheet to determine a low price for a small-cap stock.

I've frequently been able to buy smaller cap companies below the *adjusted floor price* even when the companies reflect a long history of positive earnings. This is the essence of buying low. Solid, small-company stocks can often trade at significant discounts to their *adjusted floor prices*—something typically not seen with solid, large-company stocks. These small companies often do not have many tradable shares outstanding. One cannot move in and out of them readily while they are off investor radar screens and being unduly punished pricewise. While time and patience are

> I've accumulated and held several of these types of stocks for a year or so while they were being ignored, and then, some sudden event has brought attention and they have multiplied ten times or more in less than a year.

required to build a position in off-radar, low-priced stocks, huge rewards can be the ultimate outcome. I've accumulated and held several of these types of stocks for a year or so while they were being ignored, and then, some sudden event has brought attention and they have multiplied ten times or more in less than a year.

A number of the small companies I've owned over the years have gone private or been acquired. When this happens, the share price typically jumps significantly (and immediately) in recognition of how cheap the stock is relative to what the company is really worth. When investors ignore a stock's value too long, it's not unusual for a larger entity to come along and seize the opportunity with minimal investment. Sooner or later, value is detected as a rule. I want to purchase the stock before the inherent value is noticed. My buying approach helps me find the valuable stocks that others overlook.

I'll share a couple of my successful stock ventures. I acquired a healthy position in Forward Industries, Inc. (FORD) during 2003 and 2004 for around $2 a share, based on the balance-sheet buying approach. This FORD should not be confused with Ford Motor Company, whose stock symbol is F. Forward Industries was making cellular phone and medical/diabetic kit accessories when I acquired my position. FORD was typically profitable each quarter during this time, and the share price was mildly below my *adjusted floor price* when I came to the stock. So I bought the stock at what should have been a low level and figured it would go to $3 or $4 a share in a year or so, given its profitability level when I purchased.

Motorola, a company that is comprised differently today than when I bought FORD, was a distributor of FORD cellular accessories. Not long after I acquired FORD, Motorola decided to bundle a FORD carrying bag with its new, highly successful Razr phone, sending FORD's sales soaring during this promotional event. FORD's profits escalated quickly as a result of this unexpected but positive development. An event like this would not have had as measurable an impact on a larger company's earnings, but for a small player such as FORD, the impact was huge. FORD's stock price climbed from approximately $2 near the end of 2004 to almost $30 by mid September of 2005. I sold my position above $25 a share as the stock price had run high enough to reflect virtual certainty in continued earnings growth. Yet, earnings growth had to subside because the Razr phone deal would eventually end, so it was clearly time to exit.

Once the Motorola promotional deal ended, FORD gave up its gains. I clearly did much better by selling at $25+ a share in 2005 than if I still held it today. FORD is struggling to reformulate its business and has experienced some significant operating losses in recent years, which have adversely affected the balance-sheet equity position. Also, by selling in 2005, I was able to invest the proceeds into other low-price stocks.

Another company that turned out to be a great investment is DXP Enterprises (DXPE). As true with FORD, the balance sheet was central to my decision to buy DXPE. I purchased shares from 2003 to 2005, accumulating shares at an average cost of around $4 a share. The company was solidly profitable at that time. As an industrial distributor of equipment and services, the company benefitted tremendously from growth in the oil and gas sector, with its earnings entering a rapid growth phase in the summer of 2005. DXPE's stock price rose from less than $7 during July of 2005 to almost $60 by May of 2006. The stock achieved a price in the upper $60s in the second half of 2008, just before undergoing a two-for-one stock split. It was around this time that I sold the last of my DXPE holdings. DXPE's growth has resumed today; if I had remained in the stock, my return would be much higher than what I realized. Yet even though I missed out on additional return, I bought DXPE at a low price initially. Buying low allowed for a huge return on this investment.

DXPE ascended to new all-time stratosphere highs recently, after spending a couple of years at prices below the former highs in the $60s. The price DXPE trades at today must be multiplied by two to adjust for the earlier two-for-one split. Doubling today's price puts DXPE's present price on an apples-to-apples basis with the prices I mentioned before the two-for-one split. When I saw the first mild pause in growth, I sold DXPE, but my holding period was several years long, based on DXPE's quarter-to-quarter (sequential) earnings growth and the improving news coming from the oil services sector, where DXPE was generating its fastest growth.

You see, earnings did not drive my purchase of DXPE initially. The balance sheet did. Earnings dictated my holding period of DXPE. DXPE gained notable analyst coverage once its performance accelerated, thereby providing investors with better insight into DXPE's expected future operating performance. My total return on DXPE was well over 1,000 percent. This would not have happened without a balance-sheet strategy that told me to buy DXPE well before it showed up on the radar screens of the broader investment community. My low-risk strategy explains why I was buying DXPE before it became an appealing stock to investors.

It only takes a handful of stocks like FORD or DXPE to radically impact a portfolio's performance. FORD had virtually no downside at $2 a share, given the value of its balance sheet when I first came upon it. DXPE had virtually no risk at my entry price of $4, again, based on using the balance sheet. The Motorola deal brought attention to FORD, and the up cycle in oil and gas services brought greater attention to DXPE. Greater attention brought greater trading volume on increasing demand, making an exit at a much higher price very easy.

A larger company, Sanmina-SCI (SANM), was another wise investment for me. I bought the stock at a time when many stocks were deeply undervalued because of the most recent recession. Although there were a host of undervalued stocks to choose from in early 2009, SANM made the short list of the most undervalued. In early 2009, SANM's balance sheet reflected *adjusted tangible stockholders' equity* of about $1.10 per share (*the initial floor price*). There was considerable long-term debt on the balance sheet, but it was more than offset by a significant liquidity position, as reflected in a strong *adjusted current ratio*. Its cash position was approximately $1.75 per share (cash / # of shares outstanding).

I was able to accumulate a significant position in SANM from the low $0.20s to low $0.30s. The stock price actually put in a low price of $0.18 a share on March 9, 2009—around the same time that some major stock indices (including the Dow Jones Index) hit their lowest points during the recession. I was able to buy SANM at a time when it was priced as though the company was nearing bankruptcy. However, the balance sheet said otherwise:

that SANM was healthy, financially speaking. The company was only suffering minor operating losses during this time of deeply depressed overall market prices. The *initial floor price* per share of $1.10, adjusted for earnings expectations over the coming twelve months suggested an *adjusted floor price* of at least $1.20 per share. Further, should profitability strongly return to SANM, the stock price could move back well above $1.20. Yes, the uncertainty of future earnings was more than represented in SANM's share price in the $0.20s in early 2009. It was, in the lingo of the stock market, a "screaming buy."

SANM did a one-for-six "reverse" stock split during the summer of 2009, meaning it converted every six shares of stock outstanding into one share. This means that every share following the split was priced at six times its previous price. So if you had 6 shares priced at $0.20 each before the one-for-six reverse split, you had one share priced at $1.20 following the split. The investor is in exactly the same position, financially speaking, on the stock. However, well-timed stock splits can help stocks trade better on the market. SANM did this reverse split to raise the price of its stock on the market to make it more appealing to institutional investors.

Remember our discussion of penny stocks. SANM was being treated like a penny stock but was worth much more according to the balance sheet than the amount it was trading at before the reverse split. So SANM needed to bring more attention to its stock, which it did with the reverse split. SANM soared to over $20 a share (post-split) by late April of 2010, just over a year from setting a low of $1.08 per share ($0.18 pre-split price from March 9, 2009, was equal to a post-split equivalent of $1.08, or $0.18 times six). While the move from the low of $1.08 on March 9, 2009, to the high of $20.30 achieved on April 27, 2010, represents an increase of 1,780 percent ([$20.3 − $1.08] / $1.08 = 17.8 or 1780%), I exited most of my position prematurely with well over a 700 percent gain for an approximate holding period of nine months. I did keep a small handful of shares and realized a better return upon selling those.

Although SANM was a remarkable buying opportunity in the spring of 2009, there were a lot of outstanding deals at that time. Many companies were being priced for the demise of the stock market. SANM's share price continued upward beyond my selling point, but it's nice when you can be ultra conservative and still make over 700 percent in about nine months.

Again, it does not take many like FORD, DXPE, and SANM to boost returns into the stratosphere. I have experienced many other successful investing ventures, but these three remain among the best. Virtually all of my major successes in the market are explained by using the balance sheet as my primary basis for identifying financially solid companies trading at very low prices. However, I've had some unpleasant stories along the way, too. Let me tell you about a bad experience with a couple of dry bulk shipping company investments I made, and the balance-sheet lessons I learned as a result.

The entire dry bulk shipping sector has undergone a virtual collapse since peaking several years ago. The Baltic Dry Index (BDI) is an index that is updated daily by the Baltic Exchange, a London-based exchange. The index is derived from, and therefore moves with, the worldwide shipping prices set for rentals of ships transporting different types of dry bulk cargo internationally. In May of 2008, the BDI reached 11,793, but fell to 663 by early December of 2008. In my view, there's no better barometer of how swift and deep the recession than what occurred with the BDI over such a short time. Demand for the shipping of goods across international waters went from full throttle to a virtual standstill. The BDI is still severely depressed today.

I accumulated TBS International (TBSI) based on my balance-sheet buying approach for what I thought was a steal at about a $10 per share during the fall of 2008. It traded over $60 per share a year earlier. I sold my position in TBSI at about $5 a share, just several months after I bought—a 50 percent loss ([$5 − $10]/$10 = −0.5 or −50%). At the same time, I suffered a similar painful 50 percent loss on Excel Maritime Carriers (EXM), the other dry bulk shipper I purchased along with TBSI.

Disappointing results would describe any long position on almost any dry bulk shipping company in recent years. While I would never suggest that buying stocks based on balance-sheet analysis is a fail-proof measure against significant losses, I will say that, if big losses do occur, the failure usually rests with incorrect analysis of the balance sheet, not with the concept. I recognize now that I analyzed the balance sheet incorrectly with these dry bulk shipping companies.

In chapters 5 and 6 of this book, I emphasized the importance of analyzing the quality of stockholders' equity on the balance sheet. Although both TBSI and EXM were selling well below their *adjusted floor prices* when I acquired them, my quality standard for adequate liquidity was not met for either company but I proceeded anyway. My solvency standard, however, was surpassed easily by both companies. My balance-sheet buying approach did not enable my losses. Poor judgment did. My quality standards of adequate liquidity *and* adequate solvency are both there for good reason.

Both companies reflected a huge excess of (tangible) assets over liabilities, making me reason that the companies could improve liquidity radically, if necessary, by selling off major fixed assets, namely their ships. What I failed to reason through was that the collapse of the BDI meant that the ships had collapsed in value too. The absolute collapse of the BDI signaled an equally harsh collapse in demand for ships among the dry bulk sector. I should have realized how illiquid the ships had become. If I had reasoned better, it would have been obvious why waiving my adequate liquidity standard would prove a grievous mistake. My *initial floor prices* derived from incorrect assessment were overstated because my *adjusted tangible stockholders' equity* numbers were overstated. This led to me overpaying for the stocks. Recall that *initial floor price* is derived as follows:

Adjusted Tangible Stockholders' Equity = Cash + (0.90 × Noncash Tangible Assets) – Liabilities

And

Initial Floor Price = Adjusted Tangible Stockholders' Equity / # of Shares Outstanding

The largest asset amount on the balance sheets of TBSI and EXM was their ships. My formula for *adjusted tangible stockholders' equity* discounts noncash tangible assets on the balance sheet to 90 percent of their stated values. With dry bulk shipping companies such as TBSI and EXM, the utter collapse of the BDI translated into ship values much, much lower than 90 percent of the stated amounts. I assigned way too much value to the ships and derived an *initial floor price* that was way too high—leading me to overpay for the stocks. As of today, TBSI has filed for bankruptcy protection under Chapter 11 of Title 11 of the United States Bankruptcy Code. EXM is struggling to survive in a very difficult industry environment.

The oversupply of ships in the dry bulk industry is analogous to what happened several years ago in the housing market. The sudden collapse in demand for houses left a glut of homes, a mound of debt, and inadequate cash inflow to satisfy the debt on a timely basis. Foreclosures and bankruptcies resulted. When the BDI collapsed, the rental rates the shipping companies could receive on their ships fell such that liquidity (cash inflow) was drying up relative to debt obligations (cash outflow requirements) that had piled up to acquire the ships in the first place. I did not properly factor the oversupply of ships into my balance-sheet analysis in determining an *initial floor price* for buying the stocks, and I paid a tough price for my error in judgment.

It could have been much worse, had I not taken my losses when I did. (My unpleasant experiences prior to development of my balance sheet strategy taught me that it is better to take a bad loss where recovery is unlikely than to go down with the ship. Forgive me; I could not resist the pun.) Yet the real irony to my large losses on TBSI and EXM is that they were completely avoidable.

Neither TBSI nor EXM met my adequate liquidity standard, an early red flag that proceeding with my balance-sheet approach to determining a low buying price would prove problematic. However, I decided to override my own controls, and it cost me dearly. Even so, the hard lessons I have learned have served to affirm, not disaffirm, my strategy. The losses I experienced on TBSI and EXM would have been avoided had I simply stuck to the controls (quality standards) built into my strategy. The losses were not explained by a failure in my approach, but rather a failure in my judgment to apply the approach properly.

I don't want you to think my buying approach translates into avoiding losses all together. It does not. Factors such as judgment and investor sentiment will always make absolute avoidance of losses impossible. Even so, the losses I suffered on my ventures into dry bulk shipping were more severe than the ones I experience on occasion while closely adhering to the balance sheet strategy. The main lesson I've learned from both my successes and my failures is this: one must *always* assess the balance sheet to discern the quality of the stockholder equity before trying to assign a dollar worth to that equity.

Since graduating from my early failures to a well-defined balance-sheet assessment approach to picking stocks, I have had many stock investment success stories with relatively few significant losers scattered in. Small-company stocks are definitely not for everyone. However, there are many small companies with stellar balance sheets. Frequently, these companies trade without analyst coverage and often without institutional ownership.

Sometimes there are restrictions on mutual funds, for example, toward buying small-company stock. Funds tend to buy a lot of shares, and they need to be able to move in and out of positions without upsetting the supply and demand equation significantly. That is, there needs to be a high degree of liquidity in trading volume (a lot of shares being traded regularly). Thus, small-company stocks, which can be pretty illiquid at times in terms of their day-to-day trading volume, are often off limits to institutional investors. However, the individual investor can take advantage of this opportunity.

Consistently following the same balance-sheet approach to buying stocks has led to large gains, far above average, in my portfolio with companies of all sizes. However, over the years I've found many more small-company stocks to satisfy my stringent balance-sheet stock-selection criteria. The small ones frequently produce larger investment gains and have done so for me.

CHAPTER 9

MY CORE INVESTING PHILOSOPHY CHECKLIST: PAUL'S PRINCIPLES

Investing with a sense of stewardship involves weighing the risks against the potential return. It is critical to assess risk properly to minimize losses. Losses in investing are not completely avoidable, because risks are not totally avoidable. However, risks can be greatly minimized by proper risk analysis. What can be avoided, however, is the acceptance of *unnecessary* risks when you buy stocks. If you learn how to assess the balance sheet properly, you should be able to better avoid unnecessary risks. When you practice buying low, you should see far fewer investment losses and, conversely, experience larger investment gains.

As my wife, Mickie, and I raised our two daughters, there were times when their facial expressions communicated that we were having little success convincing them of some message we wanted them to embrace. We could try to persuade them, but their faces said, "Mom and Dad, it all sounds good, but we simply aren't convinced yet." In this book, I'm laboring to sell the balance sheet as the key to buying low and hope that I'm convincing enough to persuade you to always include the balance sheet as foundational to your buying strategy. You *can* learn how to assess the balance sheet—and doing so is essential to perfecting the practice of buying low.

My approach to buying stocks recognizes that risk is always inherent in common stock investments. In chapter 11, I provide a worksheet, the Adjusted Floor Price Scorecard, to capture the quantitative balance sheet data needed to determine the *initial floor price* and then to capture the EPS data needed to adjust the *initial floor price* into the *adjusted floor price*. The *adjusted floor price* is the output of my approach and represents the price at which (or below) I may be willing to buy a common stock.

Without doubt, numbers alone can't tell us everything. There are also qualitative factors that will affect one's investing philosophy. The qualitative factors that form my core investing philosophy are those which contribute to buying quality stocks at low prices. In this chapter, I want to share my commonsense checklist of qualitative factors. The checklist has helped me avoid losses and improve returns. My checklist represents important practices to incorporate into stock investing and is a result of what I have learned from investing in the stock market over the years.

Core Investing Philosophy Checklist: Paul's Principles
1. Always analyze the balance sheet first.
2. Read what you can find concerning the outlook for the company's business. A company may be priced low relative to its balance sheet because the outlook for its industry is declining demand. Ideally, you would favor quality companies that are priced low but that have reasonable prospects of remaining profitable and growing over the long-term future.
3. Only invest in individual foreign (non-US) companies when you are completely comfortable with the accuracy of the financial statements; foreign companies, especially smaller ones, may not require the same regulatory scrutiny of the financials as imposed on US companies.

4. Avoid buying stocks on margin. Buying on margin means borrowing from your broker against your existing investments to purchase additional stock.

5. Keep some of the funds you designate for buying individual stocks available at all times to take advantage of unusual buying opportunities. Having all of your funds invested means having to sell stocks you presently own to seize the unusual opportunity.

6. If a quality stock you want to buy trades down to the *adjusted floor price*, buy half of your desired position initially. Give yourself several weeks to buy the remainder at lower prices, should the price trade even lower. Buy another 25 percent of your desired position if the stock drops 5 percent from your initial buying point; then buy the remaining 25 percent if the stock drops 5 percent from the second buying point. If, over several weeks, the price does not drop to the point at which you can get your entire desired position, either buy the remainder at the existing price, so long as the price is still at or below the *adjusted floor price*, or be content with the shares you were able to acquire.

7. To sufficiently diversify your stock portfolio such that you are not overly dependent on the performance of any particular stock, you want to own ten to fifteen stocks. You probably don't want to own more than fifteen different stocks at any one time since the oversight of a larger number of stocks can require a significant time commitment. My personal norm has been ten stocks at one time, although I have held up to twenty at a time (not recently). I have found that ten works best after years of working with my buying strategy. Fewer stocks require less time to oversee. Owning enough stocks to be adequately diversified is your goal.

8. Keep in mind that even if you do your homework on a company before buying its stock, it is unwise to put all your money on any one stock. There are simply too many things that might go wrong to place excessive reliance on

any given company. So many unforeseen, adverse events are possible, including the loss of a major customer or the untimely death of the CEO. Events such as these could reap havoc on a company's outlook. Again, a portfolio of ten to fifteen stocks is a good rule of thumb.

9. Putting an equal amount of money into each stock may not be the best buying approach. If you know you are buying quality stocks at their *adjusted floor prices*, you have a basis for believing you are buying each stock at a low price. That is, each of your stocks is a good buy. However, some of the companies may have stronger near-term growth prospects based on what you can find out about them. It makes sense, then, to overweight those companies, based on the strength of their future performance prospects, by putting more money into them compared to others in your portfolio.

10. Resist buying companies that have received press coverage that indicates a potential problem with bookkeeping or accounting. There may be news of shareholder lawsuits, for example, against the company, challenging its recordkeeping. In such cases, avoid the temptation to buy, even if the stock price is well below your *adjusted floor price*. If the stock price seems too good to be true, it may be due to a problem with the integrity of the accounting numbers. If the numbers are unreliable, your analysis has no meaning.

11. Be disciplined in buying stocks. Make use of "limit orders" to resist buying above the *adjusted floor price*. A limit order is where you tell your broker the price you want to buy shares at or below. If you trade online, you can input your buy limit order using that venue. Let's say the current stock price is $10.50 a share on a stock of interest. A "buy limit order" for 500 shares set at $10 a share, for example, means that you will buy up to 500 shares if the price drops to $10 a share or below. The limit order

is automatically triggered when the price drops to your desired buying target.

Limit orders can be entered for a day or as good till cancelled (GTC). A day limit order will automatically be cancelled at the end of the trading day. GTC limit orders, in most cases, are cancelled by brokerage firms after thirty to ninety days. By using a GTC order, you don't need to watch a stock of interest so closely to attain at your desired price. However, GTC limit buy orders make you vulnerable to buying a stock after a horrible event that would change your mind about the stock of interest. So limit orders are helpful in buying stocks at your desired buying points, but it is still wise to monitor the company news fairly often on stocks of interest. My practice is to use day limit orders and simply renew them each morning when I'm trying to accumulate a new stock.

Note that the mechanical details for placing a stock order, including how to enter limit orders, is beyond the scope of this book. Whether you invest through a brokerage representative, or online, you will have to have a brokerage account with some entity to invest in stocks. Utilize that entity's staff to gain an understanding of how limit orders are handled within that brokerage firm.

12. Always be conservative when blending (adding) expected EPS with your balance-sheet *initial floor price* to find an *adjusted floor price* where you are willing to buy. To buy low, you have to be conservative with all your practices. If you miss out on a particular stock because it does not drop to your desired buying price, there will be other stocks that will meet your price. My practice is to add twelve months' EPS to my *initial floor price* to find my buying price, known as the *adjusted floor price.*

13. When your low-price target to buy is reached, expect the existing market sentiment toward the stock to be negative. If the stock is bottoming out, don't expect any talk surrounding the stock to sound optimistic. The invest-

ment community is comfortable going with the crowd, not against it.

14. As a rule, a company with a longer history is less risky, all other things equal.

15. Read about the history of the company before taking a position—especially about the management. There is a lot of good information available on the Internet. Investigate the CFO's history. How many years of experience are indicated? Where has he or she previously worked? Is the CFO a certified public accountant (CPA)? If so, this is a positive. Has the CFO previously worked with an established and well-respected public accounting firm that engages in auditing services? If so, this is a positive.

16. A long history of company profitability is a positive.

17. "Story stocks" often have little economic substance and should generally be avoided. A story stock is when a company has a potential product or service that, though unproven, *could* transform the way things are done in the future. Stocks with great stories but little financial substance may make you some real money if you time them just right or the story becomes a reality, but if you want to consistently generate returns, you must avoid losses. The best way is to follow the admonition of this book by analyzing the balance sheet before buying any common stock and always buy value. Avoiding buying stocks above their *adjusted floor prices* will generally exclude story stocks from becoming part of your portfolio.

In concluding this chapter, I'll sum up the essence of my investing philosophy. Whether the investment is a stock, a certificate of deposit (CD), a bond, and so on, I want to achieve a return on my investment and avoid losing the principal amount of my investment. I don't think many stock investors think about the amount put into a stock as their invested principal, but thinking about it in this manner makes me approach buying stocks with the same mind-set I have toward buying a CD, for example.

When I buy a CD, I don't expect to lose my principal, and when I buy a stock, I don't *plan* to lose my principal. Just because the principal amount of your stock investment—the amount you paid for the stock—is not guaranteed by the FDIC as with CDs, or secured by any of the specific company assets that is often true of investments in corporate bonds, this should not translate into a notion that the security for the principal investment made into a common stock is completely unknown. The risk of loss to my stock principal is no doubt significantly greater than in a CD investment, but I can still practice proper risk analysis to minimize the risk to the invested amount.

It is true that a CD does not, at any time, become worth less than its principal, and it is equally true that any person regularly investing in stocks will see the share price fall below what he or she paid at times. The point I'm making is that one can still protect invested dollars by looking at those dollars as invested principal to be protected, and then buying low enough to expect not only recovery in share price but also eventual attractive gains.

Assessing the balance sheet is about protecting the amount you pay for a common stock against loss. Only then can you truly buy a stock for the return you can achieve. Only then can you review potential earnings and potential earnings growth in the right context. Remember this: if you don't analyze the balance sheet before buying a common stock, you might as well be gambling—because you are taking unmeasured risk. Sooner or later, you will experience significant losses that could have been avoided. Before going to chapter 10, I'll provide an abbreviated version of my core investing philosophy checklist.

> Remember this: if you don't analyze the balance sheet before buying a common stock, you might as well be gambling— because you are taking unmeasured risk. Sooner or later, you will experience significant losses that could have been avoided.

Paul's Principles in Brief

1. Always analyze the balance sheet first.
2. Read about the outlook for the company's industry: avoid when the industry is in decline.
3. Exercise added caution when investing in non-US stocks.
4. Don't buy stocks on margin.
5. Keep some cash for unexpected opportunities.
6. Buy half of desired shares at *adjusted floor price*—you might get the remainder for less.
7. Ten to fifteen stocks is a good number to own.
8. Don't put all your money in one stock.
9. Weight the amount invested in each stock by its relative value and potential.
10. Avoid companies with publicized accounting problems.
11. Never be anxious to buy: stick with your buying strategy.
12. Be conservative when adding future earnings to your *initial floor price*.
13. When it's time to buy, expect the market sentiment to be negative toward the stock.
14. The longer the company has been around, the better.
15. Read up on a company before buying; read management profiles, especially the CFO.
16. A long history of profitability is a plus.
17. Avoid buying a great story that does not meet your *adjusted floor price* requirement.

CHAPTER 10

FISHING FOR GOOD BUYS, PART I

This chapter and the next collectively address how to apply the balance-sheet strategy for buying low by utilizing online tools to first screen for potentially low-priced stock investment candidates and then to analyze the candidates for the purpose of identifying which stocks are worth buying and at what prices. Chapters 10 and 11 turn the language of this book into practice. It is important to focus on the processes involved in screening a large pool of stocks into a small pool and then in analyzing a particular stock from the smaller pool. This chapter addresses how to screen. The next chapter addresses how to analyze.

A website, Financial Visualizations (www.finviz.com), is used to illustrate how to screen for stocks and in the next chapter to enable the completion of analysis required by my Adjusted Floor Price Scorecard. Financial Visualizations offers the information needed with my approach for free. It is not the only online site to gather information, but it is an excellent one. After you learn the process to screen for stocks and to complete my scorecard, you can adapt the process to a different online service if you prefer. While many online stock information providers offer useful information free to the public, you can typically choose to pay for upgradable "optional" services within these venues. However, the information required to follow my buying approach is accessible, at this time, from various online venues, without a paid subscription.

The small pool of specific company stocks that you derive from screening will change depending on what date you perform the screen, even if you use identical filtering criteria every time you screen for stock investment candidates. Why? Many of the screening criteria are based on the current stock price at the time of the screen. Since stock prices change from trading day to trading day, the small pool of stocks we derive by filtering from the large pool of stocks on the market will contain a different batch of company stocks that pass our screen on any given trading day. Remember, we are trying to find good stocks that are priced low. Consider a company stock that traded for $10 a share, for example, a month ago, but today trades for $15 a share. Well, the stock may have passed our low-priced screening criteria a month ago but might not today. Under my approach, the steps you follow to screen are identical, *whenever* you screen.

The process one follows in investing must be reliable and tested by time. There are an immeasurable number of alternative investment strategies out there, and some of these surely work consistently. My reason for sharing my buying strategy is that it has consistently worked for me. Buying by the balance sheet is simply logical. I believe many individual investors perform poorly in the stock market because they do not develop a rational strategy and stick to it. If they don't see the results they want in short order, they rearrange their entire approach. The resulting portfolio's performance is total instability.

As you know by now, I tend to favor smaller cap stocks that are off radar and

> I believe many individual investors perform poorly in the stock market because they do not develop a rational strategy and stick to it. If they don't see the results they want in short order, they rearrange their entire approach. The resulting portfolio's performance is total instability.

have a higher probability of massive returns, percentagewise, relative to larger company stocks that are more widely known and actively traded on the stock market. It is easier to find a small company experiencing profitability and supported by a high-quality balance sheet with its stock trading near or even below the tangible equity per share than it is to find a large company trading at such a low level. So my balance sheet approach is going to filter out most large companies from buying consideration.

My screening criteria could certainly be relaxed to allow for more potential stock investment candidates, which would permit some large companies to qualify using the screening criteria. However, stocks would then be purchased at prices that are not as undervalued as those that pass my standards. Of course, this would diminish the return potential and, conversely, increase the risk of loss.

Before presenting my screening steps, let me illustrate why most large companies will not pass my balance-sheet screen for low-priced stock candidates. Consider the Coca-Cola Company; its stock symbol is KO. In spring of 2012, KO's stock price is about $77 per share.[3] Its balance sheet, dated March 29, 2012, reveals total equity (i.e., book value) per share as $14.54 per share and tangible equity (book value) per share as $2.18. The market's approach to pricing of KO is typical of the pricing on most large-company stocks. These big companies trade on earnings performance with little emphasis placed on balance-sheet worth.

KO has been "discovered" by the stock market decades ago, and, so long as it keeps generating solid profits from quarter to quarter, the market is unlikely to become concerned about any price that represents the balance-sheet floor. Stated simply, one is highly unlikely to be able to acquire a large company at a price that meets my strategy's definition of low.

It's time to build on this balance-sheet foundation by finding low prices on some real companies. First, we will screen for some stocks that fit my buying profile. It would be helpful if you are at a computer with Internet access. This chapter will be hands-on,

---

[3] KO did a two-for-one stock split during August 2012.

followed by explanation, followed by hands-on, and so on until we finish chapter 11. So you may not wish to continue until you have some time (perhaps a couple of hours) to spare. If you wish, you can glean what you can without being at the computer, but you will need to return to this point in the book and continue through chapter 11 while at a computer with Internet connectivity in order to attain, in good measure, what is involved in applying my balance-sheet buying approach.

Permit me to address a potential issue. I have used the Financial Visualizations website (www.finviz.com) for quite some time and always been able to follow the steps exactly as I describe below to evaluate stocks. I like the convenience of the layout of finviz.com. However, what if Finviz modifies its website later such that my play-by-play in this book no longer fits precisely? To atone for this possibility, please visit www.choosestockswisely where I plan to provide any updates to maintain the clean flow of the explanation here. Actually, while my steps below are detailed for purpose of careful explanation, most websites today are easy enough to navigate so long as you know what you need to find. In this chapter, I reveal what you need to find when screening for stocks under my approach. In chapter 11, I reveal what is needed to complete my Adjusted Floor Price Scorecard.

If you are ready, let's go to the Financial Visualizations website at http://www.finviz.com. Once there follow these steps:

- Find and click on "Screener." (It is found just under where you see FINVIZ.com on the left upper part of page.)
- Look down the left side of the page, and you will see "Filters: 0." Look across the "Filters: 0" line, and you will see that the word "Descriptive" is highlighted. Underneath this line, you will see three rows of descriptive filters, five filters on each row for a total of fifteen descriptive filters. Notice that each filter has the word "Any" by it. Clicking on the drop-down box by a filter will show you the choices for that filter. Don't choose a filter yet.
- On the Filters line where you see "Descriptive" highlighted, note that you can also select, "Fundamental," "Technical," or "All." Click on the "All" option.

- The "All" option brings up all the filtering options on one page; that is, the "Descriptive," Fundamental," and "Technical" filters together on a single page.
- Look just below the extensive box of filters, and you will see a list of stocks in alphabetical order. Just above the list of stocks, be sure and note the word "Total." To the right will be a number. That number signifies the universe of publicly traded stocks. As I look today, the total number is 6,865. There are additions and deletions of companies as time passes, so the number you see will likely be different. The second number just to the right of the number beside "Total:" will have a # sign in front of it.

If it says #1, it means that the page you are on starts with the first stock out of the Total list. If it says #21, for example, the page you are on starts with the twenty-first stock out of the Total list. The Total list of stocks is alphabetized by stock symbol. The large number of "Total" stocks will decline as you apply filters for finding stocks that meet your selected buying criteria. We are now about to apply the filters I use in my buying approach. *Remember to pause after each new filter you select to allow for the filter to be applied; when applied, the page will refresh and the total number of stocks will decline.*

- Now look at the filters. Starting with the first column of filters, find the one that shows *P/B*. Click on the pull-down arrow in the box to the right of P/B, and select "Under 1." In short order, notice how the page refreshes with a reduced list of stocks that meet your P/B filter. Look back at the "Total" for the number of stocks remaining and you will see that it has gone down dramatically. Each time you select another filter, your list of stocks will be further reduced.

With regard to the P/B, P refers to the current trading price per share of the stock, while the B refers to the book value (equity) per share from the most recent balance sheet. The P/B ratio is relating the current stock price to the balance-sheet worth. Based on everything written thus far, I hope you can see the significance of this filter. This is a balance-sheet filter, and the

"Under 1" means that we are looking for stocks that are trading below their balance-sheet equity values. Remember, you want to buy low. We want to buy near the balance-sheet floor.

- Continuing down the first column, the next filter you will select is the "Quick Ratio." Select "Over 0.5." The quick ratio is a modification of the current ratio and is another balance-sheet filtering criterion. It deducts the company's inventory balance from the total current assets and then divides the remaining current assets (regarded as "quick assets" since they are viewed as being convertible into cash quickly) by the current liabilities. I'm looking for a company that has over half the amount of its current liabilities covered by non-inventory current asset accounts, such as cash and accounts receivable, since these are more liquid than inventory. Certainly, cash is more liquid!

- Moving over to the second column of filters, click on the pull-down feature next to *P/E* and select "Low (<15)." The P/E refers to stock price divided by earnings per share (EPS). The stock price refers to the current trading price for the stock. EPS represents the earnings per share of the company for the past twelve months of reported earnings. Recall the past twelve months is referred to as trailing twelve months (TTM) in the stock market. Earnings are extracted from each of the past four quarters' earnings reports, summed, and then determined on a per share basis by dividing the earnings by the most recent number of stock shares outstanding.

In general, a lower P/E suggests a less costly stock. That's because the price is lower relative to the earnings generated by the company. A P/E of 10 or less is seen by the market to suggest a low-priced stock as a general rule. Since, I want to buy primarily based on the balance sheet and not based on earnings, I'm using a less stringent P/E of 15 or less. That is, I want the price to be very low relative to the balance sheet first and foremost. Then I want the company to be profitable. The likelihood of buying low is significantly increased if the price of the stock is close to the balance sheet worth—and the company is reflecting decent profitability over its recent past.

The P/E is an earnings-based criterion, and I'm using it as a secondary screen to the balance sheet. I would love a P/E under 10, but if I choose that level of stringency alongside my balance sheet requirement of a P/B of "Under 1," I'll effectively reduce my remaining pond of stocks to a level that would better describe a puddle. I'm picky, but I want to leave something to pick from. Please note that when the overall market is performing strongly, I often relax this P/E filter to "Under 20" from "Low (<15)" so my screen will reveal more potentially low-priced stocks. Again, my buying practice is primarily concerned with deriving value based on the balance sheet, not based on earnings, so marginally relaxing this earnings criterion, namely the P/E, does not compromise my approach.

- Look over to the fourth column of filters and, from the dropdown by *Insider Transactions,* select "Over +5%." This criterion means that, over the past six months, insiders have increased their net positions in the stock by over 5 percent. This implies insider purchases over the previous six months which, in turn, implies that insiders view the stock price as low. I like to be buying with the insiders, not buying when they are selling.
- The next filter you want to locate is *Country.* When you locate it, select "USA" from the drop-down list of countries. Financial regulation in the USA is generally viewed as stronger than for other countries, and you need to be able to depend on the numbers you analyze. So this filter excludes all foreign companies trading on US stock exchanges. While we have all witnessed financial reporting scandals among US companies, the problem is still not as widespread as in some other parts of the world. Also, if you live in the United States, you are, in most cases, physically closer to a company's home base, which can lend to your ability to verify its existence and the authenticity of its operations.
- Next, find the filter *P/S,* and select "Under 1" on the pull-down feature. Just as the P/E ratio is determined by dividing the current price of the stock per share by the EPS for the TTM period, the P/S is determined by dividing the current stock price

per share by the sales per share for the TTM period. I'm using a P/S filter of "Under 1" to find stocks that trade at a price per share that is below the TTM sales per share.

Years of investing in the stock market have taught me that companies that are being valued by the stock market for less than their annual sales are generally low-priced. However, the stock price may be low for just cause and therefore not a stock to buy. That's why I'm using multiple filters in addition to P/S. It is also why I must carefully analyze the balance sheet of any company, even after it passes all my filters.

> **Remember, you want to buy a low-priced stock when there is no reasonable basis for the price being low as it is.**

Remember, you want to buy a low-priced stock when there is no reasonable basis for the price being low as it is.

- There is one more filter under my buying strategy. That filter is the *Current Ratio*. After clicking on the pull-down arrow next to it, click on "Over 2." The current ratio is another balance-sheet screen, and we have previously discussed the current ratio. As a measure of liquidity for day-to-day operations, I'm looking for a company that can pay off the bills coming due over the next year more than two times over. I like a comfortable liquidity position. Why would you invest in a company that is strapped for liquidity?

There are many other filters at the Finviz website that we did not use. However, I've used the filters that are most fitting relative to my approach to buying stocks. Much time honing my approach has led to a set of filters that works for me. At this point, I'm just trying to get to a pool of stocks that may be worth analyzing by looking at the asset and liability detail on the balance sheet. Today, eighteen stocks passed my screen from 6,865 total stocks. The number of company stocks that remain depends on *when* you perform the screen since a company's financial numbers change every quarter and stock prices change with each trading day.

Note that all of the foregoing ratios with price in the numerator (P/B, P/E, P/S) reflect a cheaper stock price, the lower the ratio. Accordingly, our stock pool shrinks with a lower ratio level to be met. With the current ratio and quick ratio, higher ratios translate into greater liquidity on the balance sheet, and the higher we set our criteria, the more restricted our stock pool. Requiring stocks to reflect net insider buying over the past six months again restricts the pool. Finally, excluding all foreign stocks which trade on US exchanges from our analysis limits our pool once again.

The eighteen stocks remaining from the screen represent a manageable number of companies to analyze and score, using the Adjusted Floor Price Scorecard (see chapter 11). Again, the number of companies that remain when you use these filters will differ. Time will have seen changes take place in the company numbers involved when you run the screen. What's important is that the screening criteria do not change. Every time you screen for stocks to buy, you will follow the same steps. These criteria search for stocks that have the potential of being the lowest-priced quality stocks at a given time on the market.

When you have completed this filtering exercise, you can print out the list of stocks that remain, or you can simply write down the first two or three stock symbols on the list.

To prepare for the coming discussion in chapter 11:

- Close your browser after printing the stock list or at least writing down the first two to three stocks from the list.
- Return to www.finviz.com.
- Look over to the right upper part of the page for the search box to input a stock symbol. Make sure that the *ticker* bubble is selected.
- Put in the symbol of the first stock from your list of stocks.
- A new page will appear that shows a stock chart of the selected company, followed by a big box of company statistics. You will use one of these statistics in completing the scorecard.

- On that same page of statistics, find the *statements* link on the right side of the page just above the box of statistics and click on that link. Do not close this window.
- Another window will open that will show recent income statements in vertical format, with the most recent statement being the first one shown. Locate the *Balance Sheet* link on this income statement page and click the link. The most recent balance sheets will appear, also in vertical format. Note that the financial statement information page you see is provided by Google Finance; that is, Financial Visualizations utilizes Google to provide financial statements.
- Make a mental note that all numbers on the balance sheet are in millions. So if accounts receivable shows 0.35, that means 0.35 million, or $350,000. Also note that the balance sheet combines cash and short-term investments as one amount. And we will use that combined amount to represent *cash* for scorecard purposes.
- You should have two windows open: one with the box of company statistics on it and the other with the most recent company balance sheet revealed. If you wish, you can print both the box of statistics on the company and its most recent balance sheet. Doing so will permit you to analyze the particular stock involved. These two pages include all the inputs needed for completing the scorecard, and the scorecard will tell you at what price the stock may represent *a buy*. You can close the windows now.

I will conclude this chapter with a summary of the directives that were discussed at length in this chapter. It includes directions for filtering stocks and then for locating a company's necessary financial statistics and recent balance sheet numbers in preparation for completing the Adjusted Floor Price Scorecard. Mark this summary of directives for frequent future reference.

Preliminary Screening for Potentially Low-Priced Stocks
(Follow these directions *before* completing the
Adjusted Floor Price Scorecard.)

- Go to www.finviz.com.
- Find and click on "Screener."
- On the line that says "Filters: 0," click on "All."
- Select the following drop-down options, *pausing* after each selection for the filter to refresh:
  > -a P/B of "Under 1"
  > -a quick ratio of "Over 0.5"
  > -a P/E of "Low (<15)" (It is OK to relax this one to "Under 20.")
  > -an Insider Transaction of "Over +5%"
  > -country as "USA"
  > -a P/S of "Under 1"
  > -a current ratio of "Over 2"

Buying stock in any one of the remaining companies following screening should not be considered until the company is individually analyzed using the Adjusted Floor Price Scorecard. The scorecard should be completed as soon after the screening of stocks as possible.

When you are ready to complete the Adjusted Floor Price Scorecard:
- Go to www.finviz.com.
- Input the *"ticker" (stock)* symbol in the ticker box on the right upper side of the page.
- A page of company statistics will be revealed. Keep this page open.
- Next, click on the *"statements" link* on the right side of the page.
- A second window will open. On that page, click on the link for *"Balance Sheet."*
- Keep this second (balance sheet) page open too.

The Box of Statistics page and the most recent Balance Sheet page have everything needed to complete the scorecard.

CHAPTER 11

FISHING FOR GOOD BUYS, PART II

This chapter reveals my balance-sheet formula for evaluating stocks that appear to be priced low based on my stock screening criteria. They *appear* to be priced low based on the filtering process we used (chapter 10). My evaluation process determines whether the filtered stock possesses sufficient quality and, if so, at what specific price it becomes a buy. This evaluation process is incorporated into a simple tool I created for identifying a low stock price—the Adjusted Floor Price Scorecard. The steps you follow to find a stock's *adjusted floor price* will be the same every time you score a company stock. The inputs (financial numbers) will change, however, each time a company issues a new set of financial statements, which occurs quarterly.

So, if you are trying to buy a particular stock at a low price and you use my Adjusted Floor Price Scorecard to find that low price, keep in mind that you will need to recalculate the *adjusted floor price* after new quarterly financial information becomes available. The price you calculate is useful only until the next set of financials is released. The new financials (which includes updated balance-sheet and earnings information) will result in a new set of inputs into the scorecard; thus the *adjusted floor price* will need to be determined anew.

The scorecard elicits key financial data that can tell us whether a company reflects a high-quality balance sheet, and, if it does, at what price it becomes worth buying. Any company that does not meet the balance-sheet quality standards is eliminated from consideration. Parts A and B of the scorecard test for balance sheet quality. Part A collects balance sheet information to test for sufficient liquidity. Part B collects balance sheet information to test for sufficient solvency. Recall that I offered numerous illustrations in chapters 5 and 6 on analyzing hypothetical balance sheets, including testing for balance sheet quality. The quality standards used in those chapters are the same standards covered on the scorecard.

Part C of the scorecard collects information needed to determine the *initial floor price*. (We also covered how to determine the *initial floor price* in the hypothetical examples in chapters 5 and 6). Part D of the scorecard collects information necessary to permit adjusting the *initial floor price* into the a*djusted floor price*. Chapter 7 discussed blending market expectations with our balance-sheet-derived *initial floor price* to find a buying price, namely the *adjusted floor price*. Again, this adjustment is done through part D of the scorecard.

Before I illustrate use of the scorecard on a real company, please note that, by visiting my website, you can easily access a downloadable spreadsheet version of my Adjusted Floor Price Scorecard. Simply go to www.choosestockswisely.com/spreadsheet and then input **TrajAS8us5** into the box requesting your password.

The scorecard makes a determination of the *adjusted floor price* with nine pieces of information that can be found using the box of Statistics page and the Balance Sheet page from Financial Visualizations. Eight of the nine pieces of information are found on the Balance Sheet page. The Statistics page is only used for collecting the EPS number. The nine pieces of required information are as follows, and I've used the exact terminology found on the Finviz pages:

- EPS Next Y (If EPS Next Y is not available, instead use EPS [TTM.])
- Cash (Use the subtotal called "Cash and Short-Term Investments" as your input number for cash.)
- Total Current Assets
- Goodwill (The account for goodwill actually says "Goodwill, Net.")
- Intangibles (The account for Intangibles says "Intangibles, Net.")
- Total Assets
- Total Current Liabilities
- Total Liabilities
- Total Common Shares Outstanding

The Adjusted Floor Price Scorecard allows you to identify a low buying price on a quality stock. The spreadsheet, attainable at my website, performs all necessary computations involved in determining the *adjusted floor price*. Believe me when I say that this spreadsheet simplifies things to score a stock price quickly. All you need to do is gather the nine pieces of data, shown above, from the most recent financial information at finviz.com for any given company. Even though the spreadsheet does the tedious work for you, it is still critical that you understand what this buying strategy is really about. Doing so will give you an improved chance to achieve personal success. I want it all to make sense to you.

Note that if you have the nine pieces of information required by my scorecard for a given company, you can calculate an *adjusted floor price* with the scorecard on any stock of interest at any time, whether it meets a preliminary screen test or not. However, the screener I run compliments my scorecard in identifying quality at low prices. Also, note that there are sources other than Finviz for the same financial information needed for the scorecard. As already stated, I find Finviz an efficient place to gain my scorecard inputs.

It's time for us to analyze a stock using my scorecard. You will benefit by being connected to the Internet. The alphabetized list of eighteen stock symbols from my screen today shows a company named Rocky Brands, Inc. on the list. Finviz shows that the company is in the Consumer Goods sector and in the Textile—Apparel, Footwear & Accessories industry. The stock symbol is RCKY. Follow me as I manually complete the Adjusted Floor Price Scorecard on RCKY.

Remember that if you, for practice, complete the Adjusted Floor Scorecard on RCKY by following the below steps, you will calculate a different *adjusted floor price* from the one I will calculate because a company's financial numbers will change quarterly. What's important is that you follow *where* I'm getting the numbers to complete the scorecard. The most recent financials on RCKY come from the quarter ended March 31, 2012. Remember to get your balance sheet numbers from the most recent quarterly balance sheet you see available for the company. These are the steps.

- Go to www.finviz.com.
- Input RCKY into the ticker symbol box. It is not case-sensitive.
- When the page comes up, look below the stock chart for the box of statistics on RCKY.
- Look at the upper middle part of the box and find the "EPS next Y" number. Today it is 1.93, meaning $1.93 forecasted for the next year. The EPS number shown is not in millions, so use as stated. Remember, if the "EPS next Y" number is not available, use the "EPS (TTM)" number just above the "EPS next Y" square. TTM refers to trailing twelve months, which means the EPS for the past year. Please note that when you perform this exercise, the "EPS next Y" number you see will be different. For now, just accept that the "EPS next Y" number is $1.93 and that you see where I'm getting it from, because that's where you will get the updated number if you choose to determine an *adjusted floor price* on RCKY at the time of your reading.
- Find the "statements" link just above the box of statistics on the right side of the page and click on it.

- When the statements page appears, find the link for "Balance Sheet" and click on it. As I look today, the balance-sheet date for the most recent balance sheet is 3/31/2012.
- Pick up the "Cash and Short-Term Investments" amount. On the 3/31/2012 balance sheet, I see that it is 2.42, meaning $2,420,000, since the numbers are in millions.
- Next, pick up the "Total Current Asset" amount. That number is 110.85, or $110,850,000.
- Pick up the "Goodwill, Net" amount: it is ZERO.
- Pick up the "Intangibles, Net" amount: it's 30.50, or $30,500,000.
- Pick up the "Total Assets" amount: it's 166.39, or $166,390,000.
- Pick up the "Total Current Liabilities" amount: it's 15.90, or 15,900,000.
- Pick up the "Total Liabilities" amount: it's 48.89, or $48,890,000.
- Pick up the "Total Common Shares Outstanding" number: it is 7.50, meaning 7,500,000 shares.

OK, now I'm going to plug these nine pieces of information into the Adjusted Floor Price Scorecard, starting on the next page. Notice how I'm simply taking the numbers I collected at Finviz on RCKY and using them in the formula-based scorecard to derive a buying price on the stock.

ADJUSTED FLOOR PRICE SCORECARD

Stock Symbol: **RCKY**   Date of Balance Sheet: **03/31/2012**

Part A. Liquidity Test for Balance-Sheet Quality
 Key formulas:
 Noncash Current Assets = Current Assets – Cash
 Adjusted Current Ratio = (Cash + [0.8 × Noncash Current Assets]) / Current Liabilities
 Balance-sheet amounts needed from most recent balance sheet:
  Current asset amount: **$110,850,000**
  Cash amount: **$2,420,000**
  Current liability amount: **$15,900,000**
 Calculation of *noncash current assets*: **$110,850,000 – $2,420,000 = $108,430,000**
 Calculation of *adjusted current ratio*: **($2,420,000 + [0.8 × $108,430,000]) / $15,900,000 = 5.61**
 Is the *adjusted current ratio* at least 1.2? **YES**
  If no, reject stock; if yes, continue with analysis.

Part B. Solvency Test for Balance-Sheet Quality
 Key formulas:
 Noncash Tangible Assets = Total Assets – Cash – Goodwill – Intangible Assets
 Adjusted Tangible Stockholders' Equity = Cash + (0.9 × Noncash Tangible Assets) – Total Liab.
 Balance-sheet amounts needed:
  Total asset amount: **$166,390,000**
  Cash amount (same as in part A): **$2,420,000**
  Goodwill amount: **$0**
  Intangibles amount: **$30,500,000**
  Total liabilities: **$48,890,000**
 Calculation of *noncash tangible assets*: **$166,390,000 – $2,420,000 – $0 – $30,500,000 = $133,470,000**
 Calculation of *adjusted tangible stockholders' equity*: **$2,420,000 + (0.9 × $133,470,000) – $48,890,000 = $73,653,000**

Is the *adjusted tangible stockholders' equity* zero or greater? **YES**
If no, reject stock; if yes, continue with analysis.

Part C. Initial Floor Price Calculation
Key formula:
Initial Floor Price = Adjusted Tangible Stockholders' Equity /
Common Shares Outstanding
Note that *adjusted tangible stockholders' equity* is calculated
in part B.
Number of common shares outstanding (from Balance
Sheet page): **7,500,000 shares**
Calculation of *initial floor price:* **$73,653,000 / 7,500,000 =
$9.82 a share**

Part D. Adjusted Floor Price Calculation
Key formula:
Adjusted Floor Price = Initial Floor Price + Forecasted Twelve-
Month EPS
Use trailing-twelve-month, TTM, EPS if forecasted twelve
month is not available.
Note that *initial floor price* is calculated in part C.
EPS data (found on the Box of Statistics page): **$1.93**
Calculation of *adjusted floor price:* **$9.82 + $1.93 = $11.75 a
share.** Buy here or lower.

My formula-based Adjusted Floor Price Scorecard produces an *adjusted floor price* for RCKY of $11.75. According to my buying strategy, at the time of this writing, the stock may be a buy at $11.75 or less. Because of my highly disciplined approach to buy only stocks that meet my stringent buying standards, I sometimes miss out on good buying opportunities. However, because of that strict discipline to buy stocks that are deeply undervalued in price to the point that my *adjusted floor price* is met, I have purchased many stocks at such low prices as to have experienced significant gains.

A number cannot tell you everything. While the *adjusted floor price* gives me a hard buying price, I'm going to consider that number in light of my core investing philosophy as reflected by my checklist in chapter 9. You should always visit the website of the company being analyzed and gain an understanding of what the company does and about its management. Read about the industry the company functions within and about the industry's outlook for growth. In other words, gain some understanding of the general climate of the company. If your reading leaves you with a positive impression of the company's future prospects, then the *adjusted floor price* probably represents a significantly low share price for an ownership stake in the business.

The downloadable spreadsheet from my website runs the calculations I performed manually above on RCKY, given the nine pieces of information you will provide. Again, you can get the required information from just two pages at Financial Visualizations. The spreadsheet will provide an *adjusted floor price* on any stock, but be sure to note whether both the liquidity standard (part A of the scorecard) and the solvency standard (part B of the scorecard) are met. If both are met, the spreadsheet will show "Continue" after both parts A and B. Both standards must be met for the *adjusted floor price* to represent a potential buy price. If you see "Stop" after either standard, the stock should be rejected from further consideration. That is, the *adjusted floor price* should be disregarded for any company stock that fails to meet *both* the liquidity and solvency standards.

Remember you can also run the screen, using Finviz, to get a list of stocks to analyze. I have no affiliation with this online site whatsoever, but it has what I need, conveniently conveyed. Again, there are certainly other financial websites that provide information on companies for free. You may already use one that you like or you may want to explore and see what fits your style.

Checking out various sites is helpful in seeing what's out there. Plus, by searching out other sites for "how to screen" with them or how to find inputs for the scorecard, you become more familiar with what you need to find good stocks to buy. You may even find that you want to adjust my screening filters to your personal taste. I have said already that I'm cheap when it comes to buying stocks. You may be willing to assume a little more risk.

Clearly, there is judgment involved in my balance-sheet approach to identifying an *adjusted floor price* where the price is arguably low. For instance, assuming the goodwill and other intangibles to be worthless and therefore excluding these asset values from consideration is a judgment call. Doing so is conservative in that it ultimately makes my *adjusted floor price* lower, and it's logical in that putting a price on something intangible is like trying to glue paper to air.

There is judgment reflected in my decision on how liquid a balance sheet needs to be. Also, my buying practice blends twelve months of EPS with the balance-sheet-derived *initial floor price*. Why 12 months of EPS? Clearly, this practice is a judgment call too.

Judgment is involved throughout my approach. It is simply impossible to eliminate judgment when investing in the stock market. My approach is logical and highly conservative because it seeks to minimize risk by identifying quality stocks trading at low prices. The judgments my strategy reflects were formulated from much time and effort. I hope you can see how central the balance sheet is to my buying strategy. Using the logical and conservative basis of the balance sheet explains my success in the stock market since developing this strategy.

If you want to beat the law of averages when it comes to portfolio returns and accomplish strong results by remaining systematically conservative in risk avoidance, I encourage you to experiment with my balance sheet strategy to buying stocks. If you buy stocks without a rational approach, you might as well be gambling. I've been there and done that, and felt bad about the losses experienced for more reasons than just the lost money.

You may have heard this saying before: *good judgment comes from experience, and experience comes from bad judgment* (author unknown). I believe this statement is a truism. My success is from having learned how to use good judgment when it comes to buying stocks. The screen I use and the scorecard capture that judgment. I'll not forget the hard lessons that brought my buying approach to be what it is today. By sharing it with you, perhaps you can find success without the same amount of heartache.

Regular success will take more than just a spreadsheet that requires some nine inputs. It will take practice to gain that sixth sense about things such as choosing the absolute best stocks and how much to allocate to each investment. I did not develop the core investing philosophy in chapter 9 overnight. You will need to personalize your allocation strategy, and that will take time.

If you have never bought individual stocks before and you plan to do so, you may want to use my scorecard (there's a blank one waiting for you at the end of this chapter). Whether you use my approach or another, make sure to follow a logical strategy and start small—and keep practicing. If you are an experienced investor but have never used a balance-sheet buying strategy, also start on a small scale and keep practicing.

ADJUSTED FLOOR PRICE SCORECARD
(financial numbers available at www.finviz.com)

Stock Symbol: Date of Balance Sheet:

Part A. Liquidity Test for Balance Sheet Quality
   Key formulas:
   Noncash Current Assets = Current Assets – Cash
   Adjusted Current Ratio = (Cash + [0.8 × Noncash Current Assets]) / Current Liabilities
   Balance sheet amounts needed from most recent balance sheet (available from the Balance Sheet page):
        Current asset amount:
        Cash amount:
        Current liability amount:
   Calculation of *noncash current assets*:
   Calculation of *adjusted current ratio*:
   Is the *adjusted current ratio* at least 1.2?
        If no, reject stock; if yes, continue with analysis.

Part B. Solvency Test for Balance Sheet Quality
   Key formulas:
   Noncash Tangible Assets = Total Assets – Cash – Goodwill – Intangible Assets
   Adjusted Tangible Stockholders' Equity = Cash + (0.9 × Noncash Tangible Assets) – Total Liab.
   Balance sheet amounts needed (Use the Balance Sheet page.):
        Total asset amount:
        Cash amount (same as in part A):
        Goodwill amount:
        Intangibles amount:
        Total liability amount:
   Calculation of *noncash tangible assets*:
   Calculation of *adjusted tangible stockholders' equity*:
   Is the *adjusted tangible stockholders' equity* zero or greater?
        If no, reject stock; if yes, continue with analysis.

Part C. Initial Floor Price Calculation

Key formula:

Initial Floor Price = Adjusted Tangible Stockholders' Equity / Common Shares Outstanding

Note that *adjusted tangible stockholders' equity* is calculated in part B.

Number of common shares outstanding: found on Balance Sheet page (at bottom).

Calculation of *initial floor price.*

Part D. Adjusted Floor Price Calculation

Key formula:

Adjusted Floor Price = Initial Floor Price + Forecasted Twelve-Month EPS

Use trailing twelve month EPS if forecasted twelve month is not available.

Note that *initial floor price* is calculated in part C.

EPS data can be found on the Box of Statistics page.

Calculation of *adjusted floor price: buy at or below the adjusted floor price.*

CHAPTER 12

A REASONABLE PORTFOLIO ALLOCATION

You have heard the saying, "Don't put all your eggs in one basket." That saying can be used with investing to communicate the importance of practicing the principle of diversification. You do not want to put all your money into one specific investment or into one type of investment (e.g., common stocks). Any investment can go sour. Few would have believed the day would come when Lehman Brothers, founded in 1850, would see its operations cease through bankruptcy. Yet in 2008, Lehman, the fourth largest investment bank in the United States at the time, saw its business come to an abrupt end through bankruptcy. A position in Lehman Brothers common stock proved a disastrous investment for those holding the stock when the company financially collapsed.

My balance-sheet strategy follows a methodology that seeks out a low stock price based primarily on the amount and composition of the company's balance-sheet equity per share. The method is heavily dependent on the existing balance-sheet equity position underlying the stock price and, to a lesser degree, dependent on the near-term expectation toward earnings. In sum, it is a conservative strategy to identifying a low stock price.

A reasonable approach to adopting my stock-investing methodology is to make it a part of an overall portfolio investment strategy. If you choose to try the buying strategy, I suggest limiting the amount of your investment portfolio allocated under the method to no more than 10 to 20 percent. Further, I would suggest starting by investing less than 5 percent of your portfolio and see how the method works out for you. If you cannot stand to see your investment decline whatsoever in value, even for a brief time, you clearly do not want to invest in individual common stocks. The important thing is to allow yourself time to grow familiar with using the balance sheet to discover low-priced stocks.

Even though the method is focused entirely on lowering the risk by using the balance sheet as a basis for buying quality common stocks at low prices, the amount of resources you allocate to this buying strategy could be viewed as the amount you might otherwise put toward the aggressive growth portion of your overall portfolio of investments. My stock investment approach has produced returns far in excess of what aggressive growth mutual funds have produced, as a rule. My heightened returns are strictly explained by the low prices I have paid for the stocks: low prices identified by the *adjusted floor price* buying method.

I've had greater exposure to individual stocks in my personal portfolio than the percentages suggested in this chapter. However, I've gradually reduced my exposure due to retirement, my increasing age, and other factors. Keep in mind that if you have stocks that increase in value substantially and quickly, those stocks will represent a growing percent of the total, thereby increasing your percentage exposure. If you experience solid returns, you don't need to start with much to end up with a substantial amount.

I believe a reasonable approach for implementing my buying strategy is to keep at least 80 to 90 percent of your investable resources with investments overseen by professional financial advisors and to personally manage the remaining portfolio by selectively investing in quality common stocks that muster the stringent standards of my balance-sheet buying strategy. Again, if you choose to apply the balance-sheet buying method, start small (with less than 5 percent) and take time to practice implementing the *adjusted floor price* buying approach.

CHAPTER 13

THE MOST IMPORTANT INVESTMENT OF ALL

For what profit is it to a man if he gains the whole world, and loses his own soul? Or what will a man give in exchange for his soul?
—Matthew 16:26 (New King James Version Bible)

Although it is the shortest chapter, for me this is the most important one. My desire in writing this book is to share the foundation for buying quality common stocks at low prices. I believe money should be managed wisely. Sound money management includes sound investing practice.

While I was in college working on my bachelor's degree many years ago, I made the most important investment of my life. Through the words and prayers of my dear brother and several of his friends, I came to understand my need of Jesus Christ to come into my life. At the age of nineteen, I trusted Jesus Christ as my personal Savior. God changed my heart and brought meaning to everything I do.

Money is one of the most discussed topics in the Bible. In the New King James Version of the Bible, I Timothy 6:10, the apostle Paul says that the love of money is the root of all evil. While the

Bible tells us that the love of money is bad, it does not teach us that money is bad nor does it teach us that God is opposed to money. Indeed, it is the love of money that corrupts. Observing the problems in our world today, it seems clear that the more we see money as the solution to all our problems, the worse things get. Money cannot secure our lives. It is a means of exchange that permits essential commerce to take place. If we allow ourselves to believe that money has the power to secure our very lives, it can corrupt us beyond repair.

God has greatly influenced my perspective on money. He has enabled me to prosper well beyond what is typical. There is reason for that I believe. If God has enabled me to do something well that might benefit others, as God's steward, I'm accountable to share what I've learned with others. So this book is about far more than just being able to say that I've written a book on investing. It is my desire that this effort helps you to make better investments and thereby generate better returns while experiencing fewer losses.

There is no formula for ensuring that losses can be totally eliminated. However, losses arising from unmeasured, careless risk-taking can be greatly reduced through proper analysis of the balance sheet. It is good stewardship to take reasonable and measured risks. It is not good stewardship to take unmeasured risks. By exercising good stewardship in common stock selections, your goal of a growing portfolio is much more likely to result than by making unmeasured choices. Perhaps the most important concept communicated in this book is that the balance sheet permits the measurement of risk. Stewardship toward investing can lead to the blessing of having financial resources to share with those who are in need.

> **Perhaps the most important concept communicated in this book is that the balance sheet permits the measurement of risk.**

CHAPTER 14

QUESTIONS AND ANSWERS

The purpose of this Q & A is to clarify certain issues that might be raised based on the concepts presented through the book.

- Does the strength or weakness of the overall stock market impact the number of stocks that pass your preliminary screening criteria? (See chapter 10.)

Yes, my observance is that there typically is a direct impact. When the overall stock market is performing strongly, more stocks are being demanded by buyers. This results in fewer deeply undervalued stocks being available. Thus, fewer stocks surpass my stringent preliminary screen than when the overall market is performing poorly. This means more patience is required in accumulating stocks when the market is experiencing rapid upswings. Even in a strong market, though, there are intermittent pullbacks. During these pullbacks, more stocks are usually revealed by the screen.

- Do you always buy if the price is below the *adjusted floor price?* No, I don't. You should always read about the outlook of the company and its industry. If the outlook is unfavorable, it is probably best to avoid the stock, even if the price is below the *adjusted floor price.*

- What is the minimum and maximum number of stocks to own at any one time under your balance-sheet approach to buying stocks?

As suggested in chapter 9, ten to fifteen stocks is a good number to own. I would not consider owning below seven stocks or more than twenty at any one time. Too few stocks can lead to inadequate diversification while too many can become cumbersome to manage.

- How long do you hold a stock?

The answer to this question can only be fully given through an extensive discussion of selling stocks. This book is on buying stocks, not on selling stocks. Recall that I buy low based on the balance sheet when future earnings are not significantly factored into the stock price. I try to sell when future earnings are fully factored into the stock price. Once a stock I've purchased is discovered by market participants for its deep value (low price), the price can start reflecting the company's earnings potential as more buyers are attracted to the stock. The stock can cease from being priced with a preoccupation of risk (downside) and start being priced with a focus on the potential reward (upside) merits of earnings. After using my *adjusted floor price* to buy, I will start putting primary emphasis on earnings-based ratios such as price-to-earnings (P/E) to target a selling price. While my buying *emphasis* is the balance-sheet worth, my selling *emphasis* is an earnings-based valuation. The holding period is dictated by how long it takes for the market to reward my stock investment for its earnings performance. Thus, the holding period varies for each stock.

- Is your next book going to be on when to sell common stocks?

If I write a sequel, it will likely be on my approach to selling small-company common stocks. That said, the major reason for my success is my practice of buying low: the theme of this book.

- How do you decide how much to allocate to each stock?

Please refer back to chapter 12 to review what I consider to be a reasonable portfolio allocation that could include my balance-sheet strategy. My method leads to an *adjusted floor price* that *may* represent a low buying price. As mentioned in chapter 9, always read about the industry outlook before buying a stock, and avoid buying companies where the industry is in decline, even if the price is below the *adjusted floor price*. A company that trades at or below its *adjusted floor price* where the industry in which it competes is undergoing strong growth becomes a strong buy candidate. If there are two such companies, the one trading the greatest percentage below its *adjusted floor price* is intuitively a better buy candidate than the other. So it would make sense to allocate more funds to the relatively cheaper company. Thus, investing an equal amount of funds into each company may not be the best practice.

However, it is best to set a limit on how much of your individual stock portfolio is in any particular stock at a given time. You should avoid having more than 20 percent of your individual stock portfolio money in one specific stock. If a particular stock position performs strongly, going up 100 percent, for example, the amount of money invested in that company may have become disproportionate relative to the other stock positions. Even if you don't believe the company has achieved its fair value, it may be wise to sell some of that position and put it into another quality stock that meets the *adjusted floor price* measure. Some people apply the following practice (I've applied it several times):

When a stock position doubles in value, sell half that position, meaning that the remaining shares are, in essence, free because the shares kept have been paid for by profit taken on the shares sold. This is a sensible practice in my view. Proper allocation depends on a stock's potential, which, in turn, depends on how cheap it is when you buy.

- Would you ever buy a stock at a price above its *adjusted floor price?*

I have purchased some stocks at prices above the *adjusted floor price*, but not often. While there are several scenarios over the years where I've paid a higher price, the typical scenario is when a company I'm already holding shares in—shares bought at prices below the *adjusted floor price*—starts to see its stock price appreciate in response to a significant improvement in the company's performance outlook. That is, noteworthy news comes along that suggests the company is about to experience a potentially prolonged period of strong growth. This means the present amount of balance-sheet equity is likely to undergo a rapid and continual incline. If you are not familiar with stock investing already, I would suggest remaining stringent in your buying habits until you gain enough experience to recognize when an exception to the rule is warranted.

- Do large companies ever meet your screener, as described in chapter 10?

Large companies seldom satisfy my screening criteria. My screen is rather strict in its definition of low relative to stock prices. My buying strategy favors stocks trading near a conservative measure of their balance sheets. Few large company stocks trade that low. Remember that you can use my scorecard to score a buy price on any company stock. The scorecard does not know

> **Remember that you can use my scorecard to score a buy price on any company stock.**

whether the stock met a low-price screener or not. So if you are looking at a company of any size and want to identify what *may* be a low price, you can find it with the scorecard. Keep in mind that stocks that surpass an initial screener such as the one described in chapter 10 have met criteria in addition to meeting the scorecard's quality standards. That is, the screener and scorecard blend really well. I suggest always screening before using the scorecard.

- Do you ever sell a stock to buy a different stock?

Yes, there are times where transitioning from one stock holding to another is appropriate. Sometimes, after you buy a stock, the outlook changes: the industry long-term outlook was favorable when you bought the stock, but conditions have changed and the outlook is becoming less favorable. Thus, the prospect for the stock price going up is lessening. Another stock, then, that meets the *adjusted floor price* criterion may be a better place to put your capital. So selling the stock that is likely to underperform in order to invest in another with a better outlook makes sense.

- When do you decide to sell and cut your losses on a stock investment?

Remember that when you buy, the outlook of the company and its industry should be favorable. The outlook is subject to change, though. The main job you face in monitoring your portfolio is to follow the outlook for the companies you hold. If, after you invest, the outlook for a company fundamentally changes for the worse, selling, even at a loss, may be the right thing to do. Putting the funds into another solid company trading inexpensively may see you recover the loss more quickly than you would otherwise by holding the former company until its prospects turn positive again. However, if a company appears to be suffering a minor setback that is temporary in nature while the long-term prospects remain strong, continuing to hold the company—or even adding to your position—would be a proper course to follow. The central issue, then, is whether the company or its industry is undergoing a fundamental deterioration in its long-term outlook. I would define long-term as greater than a year.

- After you purchase a stock, do you reevaluate its *adjusted floor price?*

The balance sheet is the primary basis for buying a stock. You must therefore monitor any balance-sheet changes. The balance sheet will be updated each quarter as a new set of financials are produced by the company, as required by the Securities and Exchange Commission. So re-determining the *adjusted floor price* each quarter for each of your stock holdings is a wise practice. The downloadable spreadsheet from my website makes the process simple.

- How often should you screen the entire pool of stocks for buying candidates? (See chapter 10.)

The answer here can depend on several factors. One factor is personal preference. You may want to run a screen monthly to see what new candidates it produces. Or you may need to find a new stock to replace one that you have sold or are planning to sell. So long as each component stock in your portfolio is solid in its value and in its performance outlook (based on its industry outlook, for example), providing reason to expect solid future stock price performance, there's no immediate need to search the overall stock pool again.

- If more people use your balance-sheet approach to buying common stocks, will it continue to work?

I wish that would become a problem one day, as it would mean the balance sheet is being attended to increasingly during investment decisions. It could also suggest that my book has sold incredibly well. When a significant number of people adopt a highly effective practice, it is likely that positive results derived from that practice may be lesser than when there are few following the strategy. It's a matter of supply and demand. However, while results might not be as strong because fewer really low-priced, quality stocks are available to buy due to greater awareness of these extremely mispriced securities, buying stocks as close to their liquidation values as possible is always going to offer better potential returns because buying low will always be the best way to reduce risk while increasing reward potential. If a mass of people start using my approach, the result might be that the *adjusted floor price* would have to be made less strenuous in terms of its discounted nature for more stocks to achieve buying status.

The important thing is that my approach defines low by the balance sheet. I know no other way to give genuine meaning to the word *low* when it comes to stock prices. Reducing unnecessary risks with investing is simply wise stewardship practice, and you can't reduce unnecessary risks without analyzing the balance sheet.

- Since you've been using the buying strategy described in this book, what are the percentages of your losers and winners?

Approximately four out of five stocks have provided gains while one out of five has produced loss.

- Why don't mutual funds use a buying method similar to what you've shared?

My strategy would not work well for mutual funds with billions to invest. There are some small funds out there that can buy stocks like I've owned, and they do buy them occasionally. These smaller funds may use the balance sheet to a greater degree than larger funds in determining at what price they buy. Well-established mutual funds buy well-established companies, as a rule, simply because the larger mutual funds have too much money to invest to limit their stock purchase candidates to the kind of stocks that will satisfy my buying criteria.

- Will your method assure me of experiencing investment gains?

No stock-investing method can guarantee success. Further, there is no stock-investing method that can stand up completely to a market in a time at which market participants are driven by panic and fear. Fortunately, history shows that panic and fear are not a perpetual mind-set, but rather a short-term mechanism. The market in 2008 and into early 2009 was driven by panic and fear. Most stocks were pummeled, regardless of the intrinsic value underlying the companies involved. Some companies held up better than others, but there was carnage across the market. As I write today, the market has recovered, but incredible uncertainty surrounds the global marketplace.

This is why one needs a long-term perspective when investing. There is not a method that can fully accommodate the fear factor. Ultimately, however, value displaces fear. My portfolio took a hit during the downturn of 2008 into 2009, but it fully recovered and went up significantly after that. My method revealed numerous buying opportunities while fear dominated the downturn. Had you followed my method and been a buyer during that time, you would be way ahead now. While no stock-investing method can guarantee success, my method is sensible toward buying stocks low and presenting opportunity for a good return.

• What is the best investment story you've experienced?

There are different ways to define best. One way would be to define it as the stock investment that brought the biggest percentage return. Another would be to define it as the stock investment that brought the largest return in absolute dollar amount. Yet another method, and the one I'm going to choose, is to define the best investment story as the best company performance overall over the years since I first used my balance-sheet buying strategy in 2003.

I've already discussed DXP Enterprises (DXPE) in the book. The stock was a buy, according to my approach, back when I first started using my approach. Since 2003, the stock price has advanced from around a dollar a share to approximately $130 a share as I write these words. It has been as high recently as just above $150 per share. (Note that you have to adjust stock prices for any stock splits, and DXPE did a two-for-one stock split, or two shares for one share, in 2008. A two-for-one split doubles the shares and halves the price per share. Thus, you have to multiply the stock price today by two to get the price that is comparable to the 2003 price of a dollar a share I mentioned above, since the 2003 price was before the split.)

I did not experience the full measure of the 15,000 percent move. However, I did achieve a significant return. The success, though, is the company itself. It is the best-managed company in which I took an investment stake, and the reason behind the investment initially was that DXPE satisfied my buying criteria. Managers of many companies today don't always work hard for their shareholders but sometimes actually behave as poor stewards of the money entrusted to them. DXPE is an example of one company that benefitted their shareholders by making the most of the resources to grow from a small company to a significant company today.

• Do you have a website where the topics covered in this book can be discussed further?

Yes, I do. Please visit www.choosestockswisely.com to find out more.

- Now that you've retired, what are your plans for future stock investing?

My *opportunity* to retire at age fifty-four, during the summer of 2010, is the result of my stock market success. The main *reason* I retired at age fifty-four was to write this book and have an opportunity to teach its methodology about investing wisely, based on the balance sheet, to anyone interested in learning more, through seminars and other venues. I've spent most of my life teaching accounting to college students, and teaching is my God-given passion.

I started writing this book just before my retirement in 2010. It has been a lengthy, time-consuming project, but I hope the effort has produced a significant contribution. This new chapter of my life (pun intended) is gradually taking me away from trying to grow my personal portfolio through investing in individual stocks. Following retirement, my desire has been to reallocate financial resources to investments that preserve capital and that can be managed with little personal involvement. I want to spend this new season of my life taking what God has taught me about wise investing and sharing it with others. I believe strongly in my balance-sheet approach to buying stocks. I plan to always maintain some investment in stocks, and you can bet I will stay with my buying formula.

- Why am I sharing my investing strategy?

Chapter 13, for me, is the most important chapter in the book. I want every reader to know how uneasy I am boasting about my portfolio returns in this book. As a fifty-seven-year-old tonight, my driving desire is to finish strong. I'm not referring to my investment portfolio, but rather to my faithfulness toward God. I realize, though, without sharing my personal stock-investing success story, my buying method would lack the credibility it needs to be taken seriously. My desire in sharing the balance-sheet strategy is due to my belief that it provides a sound stewardship approach to managing investment dollars wisely. I believe all our resources, not just money, come from God and should be employed wisely.

There are people who espouse stewardship techniques for budgeting resources wisely and for avoiding personal debt or digging out of it. This is a good thing. My desire is to contribute by addressing a stewardship technique for investing resources into common stocks according to a careful, risk-minimizing approach. I've taught the balance sheet to accounting students for years now. (I still teach part-time even though I'm retired from a full-time standing.) God has shown me how to manage my investing dollars more wisely, based on using the balance sheet, and granted me much success in terms of investment returns. I want to share this approach with you because I hope, as a result of learning more about the vital, useful information found on the balance sheet, you can become a better steward of the funds you put into the stock market.

36909879R00100

Made in the USA
Lexington, KY
09 November 2014